Who Is GOD and Why Should I Listen to HIM?

CHRISTINE KRULAN

Who Is
GOD
and
Why Should I
Listen to
HIM?

Who Is God and Why Should I Listen to Him?

ISBN: 978-1-966596-20-2 *paperback* / 978-1-966596-21-9 *epub*

Editing, formatting, and design services by ChristianEditingandDesign.com.

Contents

Introduction

God. It is a simple word, a mere three letters and one straightforward syllable. When spoken, "God" easily rolls off the tongue. But, in any language, there is hardly a more complex word. God is a spirit. So, how do we who live in a physical world begin to define or describe him? How can we relate to a being we cannot see, hear, or touch?

The definition is made even more challenging to pinpoint by the fact that this simple word holds a variety of meanings based on individual experience. Some will say there is no God, so the word is meaningless. Others see themselves as the god of their existence who determine their own destinies. Some believe there is an Ultimate Being called God who has little to do with their daily lives. Yet others have built their lives around who they believe God to be. They choose to follow him, sometimes at a significant cost.

Early American history gives us a fitting example of people willing to risk everything for their devotion to God. A newly discovered continent offered the hope of religious freedom that beckoned these followers to sail across the dangerous waters of the Atlantic Ocean and settle in an untamed land. In the 1500s, French Huguenots fled Europe and established a colony in Fort Carolina to practice their faith freely. During the 1600s, the Pilgrims came to the New World aboard the Mayflower in search of this same freedom. A brief time later, the Puritans followed and established colonies in the New England area.

As the fledgling country grew, it became evident that religious freedom and Christian practices were vital to the early American way of life. Several documents give us insight into the hearts and minds of these settlers.

In 1620, the Pilgrims drafted the Mayflower Compact, which stated that this new colony was established "for the Glory of God and the advancement of the Christian Faith." The Founding Fathers established a unique government designed to protect God-given rights. Christian principles, such as the dignity and value of every human being, are found throughout the Declaration of Independence and the US Constitution. In the Declaration of Independence, for example, the Founding Fathers declared,

> We hold these truths to be self-evident, that all men are created equal, that they are endowed by their Creator with certain unalienable Rights, that among these are Life, Liberty and the pursuit of Happiness.[1]

Religious freedom was so vital to early American life that Thomas Jefferson drafted a bill specifically designed to protect it. On December 15, 1794, this bill was adopted as the First Amendment, establishing the separation of church and state, thereby prohibiting the federal government from making laws to establish a religion. It also prohibited the government from interfering with a person's religious beliefs or practices.[2] God truly meant something to the early Americans. "In God We Trust" became the official motto of the United States, and despite much controversy, that motto remains on American currency today. The Pledge of Allegiance to the American flag includes the phrase "One Nation Under God," and the national anthem contains references to God. The US Constitution recognizes these rights in the Bill of Rights, stating that they are God-given and cannot be taken away by any government.

Personal notes written by early American leaders give insight into God's role in their lives. When George Washington proclaimed a National Day of Thanksgiving, he wrote,

> Whereas it is the duty of all nations to acknowledge the providence of Almighty God, to obey his will, to be grateful for his benefits, and humbly to implore his protection and favor.[3]

In 1785, in Memorial to Remonstrance Against Religious Assessment, James Madison wrote,

> It is the duty of every man to render to the Creator such homage. Before any man can be considered as a member of Civil Society, he must be considered as a subject of the Governor of the Universe.[4]

Patrick Henry is famous for his spirited "Give me liberty or give me death" speech at the 1775 Virginia Convention. His passionate words stirred the early Americans to unite and declare independence from Great Britain. In a more private moment, he wrote a touching legacy to his family in his last will and testament.

> This is all the inheritance I give to my dear family. The religion of Christ will give them one which will make them rich indeed.[5]

A few years ago, I visited Red Hill, Patrick Henry's home in Brookneal, Virginia. While there, I spoke to several of his descendants and learned that they have continued to devote their lives to God. They have also established the Red Hill Foundation to preserve Patrick Henry's history and legacy.

These examples indicate that God was central in the lives of many early Americans. Fast-forward to present-day America, and we can see that the word "God" has taken on a new meaning. It has become synonymous with a judgmental attitude, intolerant behavior, or a politically incorrect point of view. The American government certainly has changed its view on God. The First Amendment has slowly evolved into something different from what the Founding Fathers originally intended. Supreme Court and lower court rulings have established the legal concept of separation of church and state. The idea is that there needs to be a wall of separation between religion and government. Now, however, the First Amendment is used to prevent religion from influencing government-established institutions. Biblical moral values are being replaced with politically correct ideals. In the attempt to maintain the wall of separation, anything associated with religion is slowly being removed. Organized prayer and public reading of the Bible have been removed from our public schools. Nativity scenes and the Ten Commandments have been erased from many of our public buildings. Terms like "In God We Trust" and "One Nation Under God" have been deemed offensive.

These changes in the view of God are not limited to politics. Gallup polls show that while 80 percent of Americans do believe in God, one out of five Americans does not identify with any established religion. United States church membership has reached an all-time low of 50 percent of the population.[6]

Only 36 percent of Americans express confidence in organized religion. Americans' views of the honesty and ethics of the clergy have dropped to a new low. In a 2023 poll about honesty and integrity among various professions, nurses ranked highest, while the clergy sank down the list. Gallup points to the evident fact that organized religion has been shooting itself in the foot. Some examples mentioned by Gallup include:

- Catholic priest abuse scandals have been recurring features in the news since the *Boston Globe* reported its 2002 series on abuse cover-up by the Catholic hierarchy.

- Southern Baptists were roiled by allegations of sexual harassment and abuse by that denomination's leaders.

- The United Methodist Church has been in the news regarding major, denomination-splitting arguments about same-sex marriage and allowing LGBT individuals to be clergy members.[7]

In the article, "Giving Up on God: The Global Decline of Religion," Ronald Inglehart discusses the dramatic shift away from religion in America. From 1981 to 2007, the United States ranked as one of the world's most religious countries, with religiosity levels changing very little. Since then, the United States has shown the largest move away from religion of any country for which we have data. Near the end of the initial period studied, Americans' mean rating of the importance of God in their lives was 8.2 on a 10-point scale. In the most recent US survey, from 2017, the figure had dropped to 4.6, an astonishingly sharp decline.[8]

What has changed in America in these few hundred years that caused a 180-degree turn in its view of God? If you google "decline of religion in America," you will find pages of articles discussing the reasons for this trend. Ronald Inglehart suggests,

For most people, religious faith was more emotional than cognitive. And for most of human history, sheer survival was uncertain. Religion provided assurance that the world was in the hands of an infallible higher power (or powers) who promised that, if one followed the rules, things would ultimately work out for the best. In a world where people often lived near starvation, religion helped them cope with severe uncertainty and stress. But as economic and technological development took place, people became increasingly able to escape starvation, cope with disease, and suppress violence. They become less dependent on religion—and less willing to accept its constraints, including keeping women in the kitchen and gay people in the closet.[9]

A 2019 American Perspectives Survey suggests that generational differences in religious upbringing have led to this decline. Young adults (age eighteen to twenty-nine) are far more likely to have been raised without religion than are seniors (age sixty-five or older). Roughly one in five young adults reports that they were not raised in any particular religion, compared to only 3 percent of seniors. Notably, the proportion of young adults who have always been religiously unaffiliated is nearly as large as that of those who have left religion to become unaffiliated.[10]

The survey explains that structural changes in the family may have led to this change. Americans raised by divorced or separated parents report fewer robust religious experiences during their childhood. Close to half of Americans raised by parents who were married during their formative years say they attended worship services at least once a week with their families. In contrast, only 28 percent of Americans raised in households with divorced or separated parents report this frequency of religious attendance.[11]

The Pew Research Report indicates that this decline is related to a series of changes within our culture. These changes are taking place for a constellation of reasons: greater secular education (college degrees), multiculturalism, shifting social mores, the secular space of consumer capitalism and celebrity culture, the sexual revolution (including feminism and LGBT equality), legal and constitutional changes (like the banning of prayer in public school and the finding of a constitutional right to same-sex marriage), the breakdown of the nuclear family, the decline of certain forms of family and group identification, and the association of religion in general with nonsensical and outdated dogmas.[12]

America has gone from a colony whose foundation was built on its reverence for God to a country where God has become a dirty word, and the trend is not limited to the United States. Religion in other countries has declined as well. For example, Europe has hundreds of exquisite churches that are a sight to behold. Yet many of them stand empty or are used as tourist attractions. What has changed? Have we progressed to the point where we no longer feel the need for God? Has God become an outdated tradition that has been traded for something more contemporary?

I believe the answer to these questions lies in the fact that we have lost sight of God both personally and collectively. As a result, we are suffering, and we need only to read the headlines for proof. Each day, there is at least one article about government or individual corruption. There are usually several articles on some form of murder, including acts of domestic violence known as murder-suicide. We daily read articles on acts of sexual violence, many committed on children. Even more terrifying are the articles on terrorism that have become too prevalent. That is just in a single day and only covers a fraction of all the violence. Despite technological advances, we are morally devolving.

If we expect our world to improve, we desperately need to find God and bring him into our lives. Without God, we are lost and drifting through life, doing our own thing without meaning or purpose. This is why it's important that we understand who God is and why he is crucial to living an authentic and meaningful life. My spiritual journey has taken me from knowing about God abstractly to living in a deep and meaningful relationship with him. This relationship, this great treasure, has transformed me. I would be utterly lost without God in my life.

The purpose of this book is to share that relationship with you. What does a personal relationship with God look like? How does it have a positive impact on our lives? How is having a relationship with a spiritual being even possible? I invite you to join me as we explore these questions together. I do not know what circumstances you are facing in your life or what motivated you to pick up this book. You may simply be searching for something more. Whatever the reason, I hope as you read that you will feel challenged, inspired, and hopeful. Set aside any preconceived notions or stereotypes you might have about God and consider the many benefits that he offers you. Then decide for yourself. Is God someone you want in your life? It is a decision that no one can make for you; it is your choice. I have experienced many blessings through my relationship with God. I want to share those blessings with you as you discover who God is and learn about all that he offers to you.

Christine Krulan

PART 1

Who is God?

CHAPTER 1

Nailing Down the Wind

What would you say if someone asked you to describe what God is like? Is he kind and good? Is he the loving Father who gives us the desires of our hearts? Or is he distant and cold, the disinterested Creator who has left us to our demise? If you could develop an adequate description, the bigger question would be this: "How do you know this?"

God is a spiritual being, so his existence is impossible to prove in our limited physical world. He lives beyond our five senses; we cannot see him, hear him speak, or touch his physical body. For some, that is enough to say that there is no God. In many respects, our concept of God is vague and difficult to pin down. Trying to describe him is a daunting task, like trying to nail down the wind. Where do we even begin?

Fortunately for us, God desires to be known. He does not hide himself from us as some profound cosmic mystery. He has given us tools to understand and relate to him. The very world we live in demonstrates

God's character because it is his creation. We can see how God created the Earth with intention and detail. He made a world that supports life and filled it with many living beings. He created the sun and moon, the land and waters, the mountains and plains. He then filled this world with animals, birds, sea creatures, and insects. Finally, he created man. He wanted a being with whom he could have a meaningful relationship.

The world God made is a perfect reflection of his nature. We only need to gaze at the setting sun or snow-covered forest to catch a glimpse of his nature. The psalmist David and the apostle Paul beautifully describe his wonder.

> The heavens declare the glory of God; the skies proclaim the work of his hands. Day after day they pour forth speech; night after night they reveal knowledge. They have no speech, they use no words; no sound is heard from them. Yet their voice goes out into all the Earth, their words to the ends of the world (Psalm 19:1–6).

> For ever since the world was created, people have seen the Earth and sky. Through everything God made, they can clearly see his invisible qualities—his eternal power and divine nature. So they have no excuse for not knowing God (Romans 1:20 NLT).

God has also given us his inspired written Word. The Bible's pages are filled with stories of people whose lives were touched by God. We can see how he took a simple man called Abram (later named Abraham) and made his family into a mighty nation called Israel. We read how God used a small shepherd boy, David (the psalmist), and made him a mighty warrior and king. He chose a sweet teenager named Mary to give birth to his Son, Jesus. Their lives show us that God is loving, patient, and kind, and that he is powerful and moves with intention and purpose. If we want to know what God is like, we need only read his Word.

We can also discover who God is firsthand through our own experience as we live in relationship with him. We learn about God's faithfulness when we come through difficult times and realize that he has been right by our side. We understand his wisdom as we apply his principles to our decisions and see the results of making good choices. We will feel his divine peace, which we don't quite understand because our world is in utter chaos. As I look back over my life, I see how his hand guided and corrected me, comforted me, and provided for my needs.

If you were to ask me what God is like, I would begin by describing his love. First John 4:16 tells us, "And so we know and rely on the love God has for us. God is love. Whoever lives in love lives in God, and God in them." Everything we know, feel, and express about love comes from him. God's love is pure and perfect. Paul wrote an eloquent and complete description of love in his first letter to the Corinthians.

> Love is patient and kind. Love is not jealous or boastful or proud or rude. It does not demand its own way. It is not irritable, and it keeps no record of being wronged. It does not rejoice about injustice but rejoices whenever the truth wins out. Love never gives up, never loses faith, is always hopeful, and endures through every circumstance (1 Corinthians 13:4–7 NLT).

What a perfect template for us to follow! This is the love that motivates everything God says and does, and we can see divine love in action throughout Scripture. God has always existed. He is self-sufficient, which means that, within the Trinity, he is complete, independent of any other being. He has no needs. So, why would he create us? The reason is that love is not meant to be kept to oneself. True love must be expressed for it to have meaning, and we know that we are born with an innate need to be loved.

We are created to be in a loving relationship with our Creator. It is our purpose in life and the reason for our existence. The Genesis account of creation gives us great insight into God's personality. Here, we meet an infinitely creative God who brought this beautiful Earth into existence out of nothing. He took great care as he made the sun to give us light, and by spinning the world, he gave us the night. He introduced variety by causing land to rise out of the water, then he created gorgeous landscapes with hills and mountains, flat lands and deserts, and oceans and lakes. He filled that world with life, fish and sea life to fill the waters and land animals to occupy the forests and grasslands. When he finished, he looked over his spectacular creation and declared, "It is good!" What a glorious thought: God created our entire world because it gave him pleasure!

God took five days to create this beautiful universe—but he was not finished. He had saved his most notable creation for last. God's desire to create mankind reveals that he is a personal being who sincerely desires to share himself with others. When he created Adam, God breathed life into the clay body and created him in his image. In doing so, he gave man a part of himself. When he created Eve, he used a piece of Adam's rib to ensure that women would also be created in his image.

In the beginning, Adam and Eve lived in the garden of Eden. The book of Genesis describes their idyllic life in this beautiful, lush garden that was filled with animals. All needs were met in the Garden, and life was simple and easy. The Bible describes how God would walk with Adam and Eve at the end of the day. They enjoyed unbroken fellowship with him and experienced his presence personally. This is a beautiful picture of how life is supposed to be. God has always intended for humans to walk in a relationship with him.

Wouldn't spending time with God in the Garden be wonderful? There are days when I long for a life that is simple, peaceful, and filled with God's presence. Unfortunately, mankind's story does not continue in the Garden. And what happens next reveals to us more aspects of God's love and character.

The first thing we learn is that true love allows liberty. God gave Adam and Eve the freedom to choose how they would respond to his love. He does not force himself on anyone. Instead, he wants us to willingly come to him in response to his love. That is why God gave humans free will. In giving us this freedom, he gave us independence. In doing so, he took a significant risk, knowing that this blessing could be easily corrupted by those who willfully chose to rebel.

Life certainly would be better if we had no choices and did whatever God told us to do. Perhaps we would enjoy an Eden-like existence. But God realizes that humans would be enslaved to his predetermined plan without the freedom to choose. His genuine love for us would not allow him to do that. So, we have this blessing/curse known as free will. And that is where things went wrong.

Most of us know what happened next in the Garden of Eden. Eden was paradise, a lush and beautiful utopia of fruit and vegetable trees and a river with four headwaters flowing through it. All that Adam and Eve needed could be found there. God gave them only one restriction: "But the Lord God warned him, 'You may freely eat the fruit of every tree in the garden—except the tree of the knowledge of good and evil. If you eat its fruit, you are sure to die'" (Genesis 2:16–17 NLT).

But Adam and Eve were drawn to the tree. What was so special about this particular tree when they had everything they could want? Was it simply because it was off limits to them? It seems so, and the serpent certainly noticed that they were intrigued. With a little enticement from the serpent, Adam and Eve chose to exercise their freedom and willingly disobeyed God's command. Perhaps at the root of their choice was the desire for independence. The serpent played into this desire when he lied to them. "'You won't die!' the serpent replied to the woman. 'God knows that your eyes will be opened as soon as you eat it, and you will be like God, knowing both good and evil'" (Genesis 3:4–5 NLT).

The serpent's deception convinced Eve, and she ate from the tree. Not only did she engage in disobedience, but she enticed Adam to do the same. But Adam was not an innocent bystander. God had given the command directly to him long before Eve was created. He knew the rules, yet he still disobeyed. Both were responsible for their actions, and their disobedience put God in a difficult place. He loved Adam and Eve deeply, but as a righteous God, he could not ignore their actions. Justice demanded that their disobedience be punished. God could have destroyed Adam and Eve. He created them, so he was entitled to kill them. But he didn't. Instead, he cursed them and banished them from the Garden.

Adam and Eve were now on their own in the harsh, unknown world outside of the Garden of Eden. Adam was sentenced to a lifetime of hard work cultivating the ground from which he had been made. There was no going back to Eden. "After sending them out, the Lord God stationed mighty cherubim to the east of the Garden of Eden. And he placed a flaming sword that flashed back and forth to guard the way to the tree of life" (Genesis 3:24 NLT).

Here, we see the drawbacks of God giving humans free will. As the painful story of Eden illustrates, our choices are our own. We can make bad ones and willfully reject the very God who created us. Adam and Eve chose to disobey, even though they enjoyed a personal and intimate relationship with him. God knew they would disobey when he said, "don't," and he gave them the unconditional right to do so. He does the same for us today. We are free to choose to develop a relationship with him or to reject him. God does not want robots; that is not love. True love allows the freedom to choose.

Unfortunately, allowing free will opens the door to sin. Bad decisions always lead to bad outcomes, but God will do everything to prevent us from making poor choices. This reveals another aspect of God's character: his benevolent love. That means God always has our best interests at heart. Not only does he want to give us good things, but he is also concerned about who we are. He wants us to be the best version of ourselves. In his Earthly ministry, Jesus demonstrated to us how to be loving, kind, compassionate, and righteous, and God will work in our lives to produce that character. Christian author and speaker Max Lucado says, "God loves you just the way you are, but he refuses to leave you that way. He wants you to be just like Jesus."[13]

God will always address sin because sin separates us from him. For example, he gave the children of Israel the Ten Commandments to show them the right way to live and to point out sins that would hurt them and others. God was not being cruel. He won't use his commandments to measure how good we are or to garner favor with him. Just as a parent corrects a child, God disciplines us when we sin. However, God's benevolent love is also realistic. He does not leave us alone and demand that we try to be good people. That is why he sent his Son to die for our sins. Not only did Jesus pay the penalty for our sins, but he also broke us free from sin's powerful grasp.

Finally, God's love is sacrificial. God gave up his Son that we might live, and this opened the door to endless potential. We can now enjoy a personal and meaningful relationship with him. What we could not do for ourselves, Jesus did for us.

This sacrificial love reveals to us the depth of God's love and care for us. It is all-encompassing, unconditional, and passionate. And each of us can experience this love in a relationship with him.

We all want and deserve to be loved and accepted. Unfortunately, because of sin, human love has become tarnished. Human love is far from perfect, and its failure is heartbreaking. Think about the child who never experienced unconditional love from their parents. How painful it is to grow up thinking you'll never be good enough! We see marriages that crumble because of infidelity. A betrayed spouse will struggle to trust another person. Or siblings who loved each other and were once close but fought over their deceased parents' estate. Can those relationships be restored?

Yes, they can—through divine love. It is the only love we will ever experience that is utterly perfect. In it, we find acceptance and self-worth. God's unconditional love will never change or be withdrawn. Through this perfect love, we will find healing, stability, and security. God always works for our benefit, which means we have the assurance that good things will happen in our lives as we walk with him. He actively works to help us reach our full potential.

I value my relationship with God because his love has revolutionized my being. Like many others, I was disappointed by human love. As a result, I struggled with insecurities and low self-esteem. I was often anxious because I didn't think I deserved anything good. I was always waiting for the bad to happen. I only built superficial relationships because I was afraid to trust anyone. My heart bore the scars of failed love.

It took God's perfect love to heal my broken heart and restore my trust. I knew that no matter what, God had my back. I gained a new perspective of my worth. I have value because the God who created the universe loves me. My anxiety has lessened because I know I can count on God. Feelings of always falling short no longer plague me. I have the hope that God will be at work to make me the person I long to be. And the most fantastic thing about God's love is that it enables me to love others more deeply. I have his example to follow, and I am learning to love like he does. I have experienced God's love, and it has changed me. I am blessed!

The same is true for your life. God's love is available to anyone willing to receive it. His love says that you are special to him. He cares about you and wants what is best for you. But it also says that the choice is yours. He will never force his love on you. It is my prayer that you will choose God's love and will fully experience all he has to offer you.

CHAPTER 2

Costly Mistake

In the previous chapter, we explored how God gave mankind free will. Let's take a closer look at free will so that we can better understand God's motivation. God is sovereign, meaning he has supreme power and authority over all. There is nothing out of his control, and his plans always succeed.[14] The prophet Jeremiah wrote, "Ah, Sovereign Lord, you have made the heavens and the Earth by your great power and outstretched arm. Nothing is too hard for you" (Jeremiah 32:17).

God always has a plan, and he always finishes what he starts. Consider Paul's encouraging words to the church at Philippi: "Being confident of this, that he who began a good work in you will carry it on to completion until the day of Christ Jesus" (Philippians 1:6).

While God is the ruler over everything, we must not think of him as a tyrant who is on an egotistical power trip. Everything that God does is motivated by love; his plans and authority are used to benefit his children. "'For I know the plans I have for you,' declares the Lord, 'plans to prosper you and not to harm you, plans to give you hope and a future'" (Jeremiah 29:11).

We know that God chose to give humans free will because he loves us. We also understand that free will is a double-edged sword in that it can be used for good or evil. When we make wise decisions and choose to do good, there is almost always a positive outcome. When someone makes decisions based on selfish desires and greed, others are usually hurt. We have all been on the receiving end of someone else's poor choices and thoughtless actions. The results can have a profoundly devastating effect on others, leaving lasting scars. We must recognize that we all have a fallen nature that is prone to resisting God.[15] There is a part of us that naturally wants to do things our way, as we demand our independence. And that is when things go wrong.

At first glance, it might seem that God's sovereignty and man's free will are incompatible. We might ask ourselves, "If God is going to do what God is going to do, why do we have free will if we can't use it?" On the other hand, we might ask, "If God is truly in control of everything, why would he allow us to cause so much destruction? Did God make a big mistake giving humans free will?" These are all very valid questions.

He did not make a mistake because God always has a plan. He knew before he created us that this would happen. Giving us freedom to choose introduced sin into our world. Beginning with the choices made in the Garden of Eden, continuing to the present day, we are plagued by our sin. We have become prisoners of it and cannot save ourselves. God did for us what we could not do for ourselves. He sent his Son to Earth to die for our sins on the cross. God made a costly choice in rescuing us. He gave up his precious Son to be a penalty for our sins. Through Christ's death and resurrection, the chains of sin have been broken. We can now live in a meaningful relationship with our Creator, and we have the power to turn away from sin. Sin will no longer have a role in our lives and the decisions we make.

Jesus Christ's sacrifice enables God to remain sovereign and still allow us liberty. While we are free to make decisions on our own, we cannot control the consequences. That is God's domain, and we cannot negotiate the will of God; we can either obey it, ignore it, or resist it.[16] God does not allow us to sin successfully. Sin only brings sorrow and death, and God will use every means necessary to prevent it.

It is easy to blame God when we are suffering and things aren't going our way. But sometimes we are in that very situation because of our sin. God is willing to forgive us, but often we don't cry out in confession before we cry out in pain.[17]

One reason God gave us this freedom is to allow us room to grow. When we make poor choices, God will use these opportunities to teach us the right way to live. God does not expect us to be perfect, but he does expect us to learn from our mistakes so that we may grow and mature.

Free will is a powerful gift that comes with great responsibility. Our choices reflect our values and character, and our decisions impact us and those around us. How we treat others matters. When we choose to be kind, we will find that kindness is contagious—creating a ripple effect that can transform entire communities. In positively utilizing our free will, we experience contentment and joy in knowing that we are helping someone else. It is God's desire that we participate in his work.

The decision to give us free will was not a mistake, but it was costly. God sacrificed his Son so that we could have this freedom. When we remember the price he paid, our God-given choices to make our world a better place take on an entirely new meaning.

CHAPTER 3

Looking Up

Several years ago on a crisp, clear fall day, I was out running errands. It was one of those exceptional days when the colors were bright, and the air was clean and fresh. Sitting at a traffic light, I looked up to admire the perfect blue sky, which contrasted beautifully with the trees decked out in the splendor of fall colors.

Suddenly, I saw a fantastic sight. Thousands of migrating birds filled the autumn sky, forming a large black column that snaked through the sky in a dynamic pattern. One minute, it would dive down, and the next, it would swoop up. It would flow to the right and then suddenly to the left. What I found so amazing was that this column was formed by individual birds flying in harmony without colliding. They remained perfectly spaced in their flight pattern. They flew in unison, knowing exactly when to dip and soar. Although there were thousands of birds, they flew as one large cloud as they journeyed to their winter home.

The birds filled the sky for a few minutes and were suddenly gone. I felt so blessed to have seen such a spectacular sight. As I continued to look up, watching the last of the birds disappear over the horizon, a car horn blew angrily behind me. The light had changed, and I hadn't moved. The drivers behind me were in a hurry to get where they were going, and it occurred to me that they probably had not even seen the incredible display in the sky. And truthfully, I probably would have missed it, too, had I not been looking up at that moment. I had learned an important lesson that day: the value of looking up.

God longs to do spectacular things in our lives, but we must look to him to experience them. When we live in a relationship with God, he promises to give us an abundant life. Jesus said, "I have come so that they may have life, and may have it abundantly" (John 10:10 NET).

Living an abundant life does not mean we won't face hardship or struggles. Nor does it mean we will become wealthy through our relationships with God. The message is that we will no longer have to face life alone. We can tap into God's resources and have joy, peace, contentment, and hope. We will gain wisdom, understanding, strength, and courage that we would never have on our own. But we cannot experience an abundant life until we are willing to slow down our busy lives and connect with God. Some people refer to this slowing down as their quiet time; others call it devotional time. I call it taking personal time to be with God. It occurs when we make time in our schedules to connect with him in a meaningful way. Here, we grow in our understanding of God, see who we are in his eyes, and learn to trust him during difficult times. We also recharge mentally, physically, and spiritually and gain new perspectives on the world around us.

Through the Holy Spirit, God teaches us how to live productive, meaningful lives as we grow in character and become more like Jesus. John 15:5 gives us a beautiful analogy: "Yes, I am the vine; you are the branches. Those who remain in me, and I in them, will produce much fruit. For apart from me you can do nothing" (NLT).

Like a grapevine, we must be connected to God. This connection provides us with the spiritual nourishment to live the way he wants us to live. Without God as our life source, we will slowly starve spiritually, and eventually, like the branch cut from the vine, we will shrivel and die.

The abundant life is available to anyone who wants to receive it, no matter who we are or what we've done. It is possible because of what Jesus did on the cross. His death and resurrection allow every one of us to have a meaningful relationship with God.

The remainder of this chapter will focus on how each of us can establish a relationship with a spiritual God. The key is having consistent alone time with him. Without it, we will know a great deal about God in our minds, but we will fail to know him personally in our hearts.

First, it is important to make your time with God a priority. This means our time with him is nonnegotiable. The Bible tells us, "But seek first his kingdom and his righteousness, and all these things will be given to you as well" (Matthew 6:33).

This does not mean that to be a good Christian, you must set yourself apart and move to a monastery. You can develop a relationship right now, right where you are. When you prioritize God, he has promised that he will take care of you.

How much time you can commit depends on your circumstances. A parent with small children will not have as much time as a retired person. The most important thing is the quality of the time spent with God and the attitude of our hearts. Sometimes, the biggest life lesson is learned when we quickly cry out to God for help and later see how he answers that prayer.

Second, be consistent. Your time alone with God is well worth the effort. God will use it to build and strengthen you. You will cultivate the habit of turning to him when you face challenges and struggles. You will learn to seek God's wisdom instead of trying to figure things out alone. Time with God helps shape your perspective, which often brings peace and comfort even when life seems like it is falling apart. Being with God gives you a sense of security, knowing that you are not alone and that God is always there for you.

Third, we must approach God with right motives. The purpose of alone time is to get to know and understand God, to learn what he expects of us, and build our trust in him. It is easy to make our quiet time a duty, another thing on our to-do list. But if that is our motivation, it will become dry, dull, and boring because it is one-sided. It will be more about what we are doing (or not doing) and less about what God is doing in us. We are just seeking to fulfill a task and are missing meaningful interaction with God.

It's worth noting here that our relationship is not just about us talking to God. He also speaks to and interacts with us. We feel his presence and leading as we pray and read his Word.

Our quiet time should not be a means to try to gain favor with God. He is loving and generous, and will give us many good things, because that is who he is. He also may withhold some things because he has a lesson to teach us or has something better in mind. Allow God to do as he sees fit and be thankful for his blessings. We do not need to use our quiet time to earn God's time and attention, hoping he will find us worthy one day. Christ has already paid the penalty for our sins and made our relationship with God possible. He sees us and loves us just the way we are. We can relax and enjoy God's presence!

Your time alone with God can be tailored to your needs and likes. It will depend on your schedule and whether you are a morning person or a night owl. The duration also depends on your personality. Some prefer shorter periods several times throughout the day. Others like to sit for a half hour or more to settle and focus their minds. Where you spend your time alone with God is also an individual preference. When the weather is nice, I enjoy sitting on my deck in the morning after everyone has left the house for the day. A woman I know used to shut herself away in an empty closet because it was the only place where she wasn't continually interrupted by her family. She would light a lovely, fragrant candle, and her family knew not to come knocking when it was lit.

While certain aspects of our quiet time can be tailored to our personalities, other elements of that time are necessary. God has provided them to help facilitate a growing, healthy relationship with him. If we are wise, we will use them regularly. These essential components are prayer, the Bible, and the Holy Spirit.

Prayer

We communicate with God through prayer. Yes, he already knows exactly what is going on in our lives—our hurts and pains, our worries and concerns. However, when we pray, we open our hearts and lives to God and invite him to be involved.

The key to prayer is to make it simple. Prayer is our opportunity to spend time with God and enjoy his presence. Unfortunately, we often make it so complicated that it is no longer about God and so cumbersome that we don't enjoy it. Joyce Meyers, in her book *The Power of Simple Prayer,* says,

> Sometimes, people make prayer dry and difficult; sometimes, our religious mindsets and "systems" present prayer in such a way that it seems out of reach for many of us. I tell you the truth when I say that God desires our prayer lives to be natural and enjoyable. He wants our prayers to be honest and heartfelt, and he wants our communication with him unencumbered by rules, regulations, legalism, and obligation. He intends for prayer to be an integral part of our everyday lives—the easiest thing we do each day.[18]

Remember that God always hears our prayers, and he responds. Even when we don't see immediate results, our prayers matter to God, and prayer has power. It changes things because it opens the door for God to work in our lives and the lives of those around us. Our strength and resources no longer limit us. We now have access to God's power, wisdom, strength, and resources. All we need to do is ask. James 4:2 reminds us, "You do not have because you do not ask God."

While prayer should be simple, having a list of things to discuss with God is helpful. I have found three key elements that have become the framework of my time spent in prayer. They keep my prayers balanced and remind me of God's character.

The Components of Prayer

Praise

Praise is a foundational building block in our relationship with God. It is not an exercise of stroking God's ego by reminding him of who he is.

He already knows who he is. Praise is about us becoming close to him and fully appreciating his character. It is also foundational because if we do not know who he is and what he is like, we will never be able to trust him fully. If we do not trust God, the relationship will not grow and become more intimate.

God is unlike anyone we have ever known. While he is mighty, strong, and all-powerful, he is also gentle, kind, and loving. He is far more significant than our imagination can fathom. Yet, he is close and personal to all who seek him. We can spend our entire lives getting to know him, and we will be just touching the tip of the iceberg. Thankfully, we will be with him for eternity in heaven.

God always stays true to his character. He remains unchanged and consistently acts in the same manner. As we know him more intimately, we can truly appreciate all he does for us. The Bible has many examples of people praising God. The book of Psalms is filled with praise and worship. In some respects, reading Psalms is like reading someone's diary. The words are heartfelt, full of raw emotion, down-to-Earth, and honest. But they go beyond just expressing human emotions; they paint a portrait of God. They tell us about his unfailing love, reveal his incredible power and strength, and communicate his forgiveness and mercy. They remind us that despite the woes of this world, God is bigger than all our problems.

I have found it helpful to use words from the Psalms as a template for my prayers. When I read a psalm, I pick out keywords or phrases that are most meaningful to me. Then I pray them back to God. For example, the first verses of Psalm Chapter 18 exclaim,

"I love you, O Lord, my strength. The Lord is my rock, my fortress and my deliverer; my God is my rock, in whom I take refuge, my shield and the horn of my salvation, my stronghold" (Psalm 18:1–2).

As I read this psalm, the thought that God is my strength and rock stands out. I begin my prayer like this: "Father, I praise you for being my rock. Although I face some tough times, I can always count on you. Thank you for being my strength." To give my prayers more meaning, I sometimes say them out loud. Other times, I will record them in my prayer journal. I have found that the psalmist expresses things about God that I have never thought of. What a blessing it is to have these recorded prayers to remind us of who God is and how he works in our lives! Although they were written centuries ago, they remain relevant today.

Studying the different Hebrew names for God is another excellent tool to help us understand who he is. This may not be easy because the Hebrew language is unfamiliar to most of us. However, the names of God in Hebrew encompass so much in a single word. For example, the word Adonai in Hebrew means that God is the ultimate ruler over all things. Everything falls under his authority. Additionally, the word Adonai conveys the understanding that the Owner is responsible for the provision, protection, and guidance of those under his care.[19] So, Adonai tell us that God is the ultimate ruler, and it describes what type of ruler he is. He is not a mean tyrant who cares little about his charges. He is a ruler who cares deeply about his subjects. While studying the names of God might take some discipline, it is well worth the effort. There are many excellent study books available on the names of God. They can be extremely helpful in understanding the different names and their implied meaning.

Confession

Another key component of prayer is confession. In today's world, we rarely hear about confession. It is often associated with confession to a priest, allowing us to receive forgiveness. However, forgiveness comes from God, so confession needs to be made directly to God. "Repent, then, and turn to God, so that your sins may be wiped out, that times of refreshing may come from the Lord" (Acts 3:19).

Confession must be a part of our prayer time, but keep in mind its true purpose. First, we are not telling God anything he does not already know when we pray about our sins. Nothing is hidden from God's sight. God does not ask that we bring our sin before him to condemn us or remind us that we are failures. Jesus has already paid the penalty for our sins, so we no longer stand before God with a guilty sentence.

The reason God asks us to confess our sins is to teach us. First, we need to recognize and admit sin in our lives. Sometimes, we become so accustomed to sin's presence that we don't even notice it. Or we try to justify our unruly behavior to minimize or dismiss our sin. We need to be honest about the sin in our lives and call it what it is, wrong. Through confession, God wants to teach us how sin hurts us and those around us. Remember, there is always a consequence for our wrongdoings. We might think we have gotten away with it and that it does not matter. There are still consequences, no matter how long it takes for us to see them. Nothing good ever comes from sinful actions.

Finally, through confession, God teaches us how to turn away from sin. In other words, how do we stop engaging in harmful behavior? The excellent news is that God does not condemn us for our sins. Instead, he extends mercy and grace as he helps us change by breaking sin's hold on us. "Jesus answered them, 'I tell you the solemn truth, everyone who practices sin is a slave of sin. . . So if the son sets you free, you will be really free'" (John 8:34, 36 NET).

He begins by uncovering the motives behind our damaging behavior. Why do we do what we do? Our thinking primarily dictates our actions, and often, a faulty perspective leads us into sin. Another, more subtle, motive for sin is a lack of trust. We do not fully trust God and his goodness toward us. Our lack of confidence makes us vulnerable to being controlled and manipulated for our gain. God reveals these weaknesses and empowers us to trust him to lift us out of our sin.

I have found confession to be a liberating experience. Over the years, I held secrets I didn't want anyone else to know. I felt immense shame and embarrassment about the things I had done, and sometimes I didn't like the person I had become. I found it difficult to acknowledge my sin and found it easier to stuff those feelings deep down inside and pretend they were not there. In the end, I was only kidding myself. They were still there, and they were slowly eating me away inside.

I cannot even begin to describe what it was like the first time I bared my soul to God. I knew he knew about all my sins, including the hidden ones, and I was worried. As I expressed my deepest secrets, I expected condemnation. I was sure God would turn his back on me. However, to my great surprise, I found God's forgiveness and love rather than condemnation. I found mercy and acceptance. I realized God did not want me to confess my sins because he wanted to punish me. God wanted me to be honest with myself so he could help me. He could not heal me or begin to change me until I confessed that I needed his help.

Laying Down Burdens

Another component of prayer can best be described by the image of bringing one's burdens and laying them down at the feet of Jesus. We've all experienced it in one form or another. Perhaps it's the financial pressure of trying to stretch our money to meet life's demands or the stress of having teenagers who want independence. It may be the struggle of keeping a marriage together while the world tries to tear it apart. Whatever the burdens, they all have one thing in common: They weigh us down. They leave us tired and emotionally drained.

The good news is that we were never meant to carry these burdens alone. We are meant to leave them at God's throne and ask him to help us handle them. "The Lord deserves praise. Day after day he carries our burden, the God who delivers us. (Selah)" (Psalm 68:19 NET).

God not only helps us carry the weight of our burdens but also helps us find solutions to the problems that overwhelm us. When we pray, we can address these issues and ask for God's help. His unlimited spiritual resources are available to us, and he will freely give them to us if we ask. Our weary souls desperately need these resources to face life's challenges.

I have carried many burdens and am learning the value of laying them at God's feet. I have been blessed with the experience of witnessing God at work during difficult times. God answers prayer. It is the only way to explain my sudden peace, even when my life is chaotic. His answer is often seen in newfound strength and hope amid a dark time. When you lay your burdens at God's feet, you say, "God, I am trusting you to help me!" That is a prayer that God will not ignore. In his timing and way, he will answer that prayer in ways you cannot imagine.

Prayer Journal

A journal is one of the best tools I use to grow in my prayer life. In it, I record my prayers and thoughts. I also jot down lessons God has been teaching me and any sins I have uncovered that need to be addressed. I am open and honest about what I record in my journal, even when expressing negative emotions such as frustration, anger, sadness, or fear. My prayer journal has enabled me to pour out my heart to God and express my innermost emotions. God is not surprised by these negative feelings and has made me aware of my inner struggles. That opens the door. With God's help, I can address these struggles.

Writing in a prayer journal is also a way to stay focused during my prayer time. I can easily become distracted by wandering thoughts while praying. Physically writing something down helps me focus and remember what I have been praying about. A journal also provides me with a written record of notable events that have occurred in my life, the trials I have faced, and the difficulties I have overcome. I often leave a space for my requests, and when God answers my prayers. I note how he answered them along with the date they were answered. It is a written testament to God's faithfulness and can be a great encouragement when facing future struggles.

The Power of Prayer

Prayer is a gift and a privilege, and I confess that I am just beginning to realize it. For a long time, I had the attitude that "God is going to do what God is going to do. Why do I need to pray?" That perspective made my prayer life dull and boring. I have learned there is power in prayer to change every aspect of our lives. It is essential to understand the role of prayer in the believer's life. God does not command us to pray because he does not know what to do. He does not need us to pray so that he knows what is happening in the world. Yes, God has his plans and purposes, and they will not be stopped. But he has done something quite remarkable. He has chosen to use people—you and me—to carry them out. He wants us to be involved in what is going on in our world.

We were not created to sit idly by and watch things happen. God wants us to work with him to improve our world. It does not matter who we are or what our social status is; he can use each of us to make a positive difference in our world. Some of us are called to find solutions to many of our social issues. Many work to encourage and build up others so that they learn to walk with God. Others might answer God's call by meeting people's needs in practical ways. Each task is essential to God; nothing is too small in his eyes. God allows us to be part of the positive change our world desperately needs. Not only do we have the chance to help others, but in doing so, we will gain the satisfaction and joy of knowing that God has used us to make a difference.

Jeremiah shows the interconnection of God's purposes and man's deeds. "Great are your purposes and mighty are your deeds. Your eyes are open to the ways of all mankind; you reward each person according to their conduct and as their deeds deserve" (Jeremiah 32:19). People of prayer are essential to carrying out God's purposes here on Earth. There is no doubt that our world is suffering, and sin is growing in magnitude. Like never before, we need to remind ourselves of the value and power of prayer. God has given us a great privilege when he asks us to pray. We can trust that our prayers are important and that God will use them for good.

Reading God's Word

The Bible is much more than a history book. It is God's inspired written Word to us. Although written many years ago, its message is relevant today—and it is still the bestselling book of all time! The Bible reveals to us who God is and how much he loves us. His Word also lays out the blueprint for living a meaningful life that is pleasing to God. It is our guidebook, our source of strength, encouragement, wisdom, and hope.

Why is reading the Bible so important? First, the Bible is the source of truth because all truth comes from God. We all could use a good dose of truth at this point in history. We have the blessing of the internet and tools such as Google with information readily available at our fingertips. While this information explosion seems great, the flip side is that we are also inundated with misinformation. We are all aware of how quickly distortions, half-truths, and fake news can spread across the internet. There is often enough credibility to make a story seem believable, but it isn't completely truthful. Thus, we don't know what to believe. Truth is becoming increasingly difficult to find, which is why we desperately need to read God's Word to understand what truth actually looks like.

The second reason we should read the Bible is found in Psalm 119:105: "Your word is a lamp for my feet, a light on my path." In its pages, we can learn how to navigate life's challenges. The psalmist recognized that living in a sinful world can be difficult and painful. He shows us here that God has not left us to fend for ourselves. He has given us his Word to help us.

Third, God's Word is a mirror that provides an accurate reflection of who we are and helps us recognize how much we need God. Matthew 5:3 tells us, "Blessed are those who recognize they are spiritually helpless.

The kingdom of heaven belongs to them" (GW). By consistently reading the Bible, we will become the people we are meant to be.

How to Study God's Word

Making God a priority takes time and effort, but every endeavor to get to know him will be worth it. Studying God's Word requires diligence and perseverance, like having a daily homework assignment. It can be something to put off because we lead busy lives, but there are enormous benefits in spending time in God's Word. All the hard work will pay off in ways you cannot imagine.

There are different approaches to reading the Bible. If you have never done so, you may want to consider reading the entire Bible to gain a comprehensive overview. *The One Year® Bible* is an excellent tool. It is set up in chronological order and allows the reader to cover the entire Bible in 365 days by consistently reading for fifteen minutes a day. Another helpful resource is a reading plan that outlines daily assignments. These readings typically include sections from three or four books of the Bible. Each day consists of a section from each book, moving you sequentially through each chapter. Both of these approaches require discipline, but they are well worth the effort.

You may want to take a more in-depth approach to studying the Bible by reading one book at a time. Books and studies are available that will help guide you through each chapter. These studies highlight keywords and concepts to aid in your understanding.

Many people use the Bible to study specific topics. This is a good approach for people who are struggling in a particular area and need some insight. For example, someone might find that they are having a difficult time with anxiety, so they do a topical study on worry.

Many excellent books on the market explore how God's Word helps us with anxiety, worry, and fear. The Bible serves as our guidebook, providing us with help on various topics, including financial struggles, relationship issues, and parenting challenges.

Joining a Bible study is a great way to connect with others while learning about God. It helps to establish accountability when studying in a group. This also allows you to see what insight and opinions others have to offer. Delving into God's Word together is also a great way to develop strong friendships. I have been blessed by the Bible studies I have attended, and I'm deeply grateful for the people who have helped me through some tough times.

The Holy Spirit

The final component of a healthy relationship with God is the Holy Spirit. We need the Spirit's presence because he is the "glue" that holds all the other components together. Without him, our alone time with God is a duty we perform. It will quickly become dull, and we will likely give up. We need the Holy Spirit present when we begin our quiet time because he is our teacher and guide. We need to learn how to listen to what he is telling us and how to depend on him.

For years, my prayer life was filled with a list of "things" to pray about. It was my spiritual to-do list, and I approached it like any chore that needed to be done. My prayer life was brief and ineffective. That changed when I discovered the secret to a meaningful prayer life, which began with these words: "Holy Spirit, teach me to pray!" It is a plea that God will gladly answer because prayer is powerful. We need to learn how to pray in a way that impacts the world around us. To do that, the Holy Spirit is here to teach us. Learning to listen to and respond to what the Holy Spirit is saying will serve us well and help us grow in our relationship with God. The power of our prayer is found in the presence of the Holy Spirit and our response to him.

The same is true when it comes to studying God's Word. If we are new to reading the Bible, we will find some parts confusing and challenging to understand. Without the Holy Spirit's guidance, it is easy to miss the Bible's truth and form our own interpretations, which are often incorrect and misleading. To correctly understand what the Bible says, we need the Holy Spirit to teach us. The Bible becomes the living Word when we read with the Holy Spirit as our guide. Its truth will never change and can be applied to any circumstance in history. It holds meaning for each individual who studies its pages.

We cannot neglect the Holy Spirit's presence. He is a special gift from God, and he is here to help us. We are not alone! We have God's great resource right here with us. I love this quote from beloved pastor Dr. Paul Bubna:

> In our own strength we will be influenced by our society. In the Holy Spirit's strength, we can influence our society.[20]

Sometimes, we become overwhelmed by the world. Moral standards are far lower than what God wants for us, and life is so far from what it should be. We often feel disappointed and even hopeless in our circumstances. Too frequently, we settle for what is rather than what can be. In doing so, we have given up on what God wants to give us. We have accepted the unacceptable and think that life is the best it can be, considering the world we live in. But God wants to give us more than we can even imagine. That is why he has given us the gift of his Word, the privilege of communicating with him through prayer, and the presence of the Holy Spirit. When we accept these gifts and utilize them to their fullest potential, we can see the spectacular future that God has laid out before us.

CHAPTER 4

Hidden Treasure

Through the years, I have noticed that my taste in TV programs has changed dramatically. In my younger years, I enjoyed soap operas. The more drama, the better. I loved watching the fighting and conflicts among the characters, the highs and lows each character faced, and the betrayals and backstabbing that added spice to the show. Each episode ended with a cliffhanger, always leaving me wanting more. These were pre-streaming days, so I had to wait a week to see what would happen next.

Now, I find it impossible to watch such shows. The conflicts that I used to find entertaining give me a headache. I laugh at their first-world problems and want to yell at the characters, "Just get over it and move on!" Life has taught me many lessons, and I have learned firsthand how challenging it can be. I have experienced enough conflict in my everyday life, and I do not want any more drama.

Instead, over the years, educational programs have become more my speed. Surprisingly, I enjoy watching The HISTORY Channel, National

Geographic, and PBS. I love learning about different places and people. I find inspiration in their stories; they open my mind to a world larger than my own experience. I walk away from these programs feeling like I have learned something useful and valuable, and the experience has added something positive to my life.

The Curse of Oak Island is a fitting example of programming that I now enjoy. The series follows the quest of brothers Marty and Rick Lagina as they search for a fabled, hidden treasure buried on a remote piece of land known as Oak Island. Located on Nova Scotia's south shore, Oak Island is one of approximately 300 islands that comprise Mahone Bay. Many believe a massive treasure is buried in the 140-acre forest-covered area due to the legends and stories that have emerged about the island since the late 18th century. A "curse" on the treasure is said to have originated more than a century ago, stating that seven men will die in the search for the treasure before it is found.[21]

This fascinating series has captured the attention of TV viewers. Unsurprisingly, *Forbes* magazine headlined "History Channel's 'Curse of Oak Island' Draws Millions of Viewers—Beating Almost Everything Else On Cable."[22] The show has mystery, suspense, and unanswered questions that keep viewers coming back for more. Where is this hidden treasure? Who put it there? Will the brothers ever find it? It also has a colorful cast of characters, like Gary Drayton, the metal detection expert. Gary has become popular with the show's audience for his interesting finds, such as the lead cross, and his unique phrases, including "a Bobby Dazzler" or a "Top Pocket Find." His passion and enthusiasm have endeared him to viewers worldwide.

The one thing that stands out about this show is the dedication and persistence of these treasure hunters. They have faced numerous setbacks, challenges, and stormy weather; yet they persist in their quest. Their passion is inspirational as we hear phrases like "there is a possibility" or "there is potential." The hunters have spent countless hours planning strategies, researching the island's history, consulting a myriad of experts, and digging even more tunnels. I admire their persistence. I would have given up by now, cut my losses, and gone home. Yet, after eleven seasons, the brothers continue. Their sole motivation is that all their efforts will be worthwhile when the treasure is found.

The brothers' quest reminds me of a parable told by Jesus and recorded in the gospels. He tells the story of a man who found a great treasure in a field and did everything in his power to acquire that property. "The kingdom of heaven is like a treasure hidden in a field. One day a man found the treasure, and then he hid it in the field again. The man was very happy to find the treasure. He went and sold everything that he owned to buy that field" (Matthew 13:44 ICB).

Jesus's account is different from the Oak Island saga in that the treasure had already been found and reburied to keep it hidden. This parable may describe the early history of the Oak Island treasure. Someone recognized the value of the treasure and felt the need to keep it safe.

In both cases, the main point is the value of the treasure. Someone deemed the treasure so valuable that they were willing to go to great lengths to obtain it. That certainly describes Rick and Marty, who have put tremendous resources and effort into uncovering the island's hidden treasure. Likewise, the man in the parable was willing to sell everything he owned to secure the treasure in the field.

What was this great treasure? Remember that in Scripture, whenever Jesus relates a parable, it may appear on the surface that he is just telling a story. But behind every one of Jesus's parables is a spiritual principle.

The truth here is that the kingdom of heaven is of inestimable value. When we believers value God's kingdom, we will dedicate time, effort, and resources to keep it secure.

While the parable of the hidden treasure is only a few sentences long, it is packed with spiritual meaning. Notice that in the story, the man finds this treasure in a field. How he finds it is uncertain. Perhaps he is taking a shortcut across the field, notices something in the ground, and starts digging. Or maybe he is considering buying the field, and upon inspecting it, he discovers the treasure. One thing is clear: The treasure was not easily visible, and it required some effort to uncover. It is the same with God. He is ever-present in our lives, but we will never realize he is there unless we look for him. He asks us to seek him, meaning he expects us to go in search of him. He hides in plain sight, and when we open our eyes and seek him, we find him nearby.[23]

As the parable continues, the man recognizes this treasure is extremely valuable. So, he quickly decides to secure the treasure and make it his own. He sells everything he owns to have the means to buy this field. And he does it joyfully, knowing that all he is giving up will be worth it. The parable then compares the man's story to the kingdom of God. The kingdom of God is of immeasurable value. When we seek and find it, we will discover it to be a great treasure. We must make it our priority and build our lives around it.

Do we truly understand and value God's kingdom? For many years, God's kingdom was the furthest thing from my mind—I was so busy running my world that I had time for little else. And I almost walked by the greatest treasure ever found!

So, what exactly is the kingdom of God, and why do some consider it a great treasure? The kingdom of God is the central theme of the

Bible, and the key message Jesus preached during his time on Earth. Prophets in the Old and New Testaments gave light to the presence of God's kingdom. It is referred to by several names in the Scriptures, including the kingdom of heaven and the kingdom of God. They all have the same meaning: God's kingdom. This should not be confused with our modern term, which describes a specific place, territory, and government. Christian author Mary Fairchild explains, "The Kingdom of God is the realm where God reigns supreme, and Jesus Christ is King. In this Kingdom, God's authority is recognized, and his will is obeyed."[24] Old Testament scholar Graeme Goldsworthy paints an even clearer picture. "God's people in God's place under God's rule."[25]

This is a spiritual kingdom not defined by time, space, or location. It has no borders, and its inhabitants are those who have chosen to believe in God and accept the forgiveness that Jesus Christ offers. It is also timeless, so all the children of God throughout the centuries of humanity will be found there. For now, the kingdom of God exists within the hearts of God's children. This will become a physical kingdom when Jesus returns to Earth and establishes his kingdom here. "So always be ready, because you don't know the day or the hour the Son of Man will come" (Matthew 25:13 NCV). In Revelation, John provides this further insight: "Then the seventh angel blew his trumpet, and there were loud voices in heaven saying: 'The kingdom of the world has become the kingdom of our Lord and of his Christ, and he will reign forever and ever'" (Revelation 11:15 NET).

Why is God's kingdom relevant to us now? Because it is how life was meant to be when he created us. He made us as an expression of his love and character. He wanted us to dwell in an Eden-like environment where we live in peace and harmony with him, his creation, and others. However, humans rebelled against the Creator in a quest for independence, and sin entered the world. And things have gone wrong ever since. The life we experience here on Earth is far from what God ever intended.

But God did not give up on humankind. He rescued us when he sent Jesus to die for our sins. Our relationship with God is restored. His kingdom is made up of women and men who willfully choose to turn from their independent ways and follow him in a relationship. They have accepted Christ's work on the cross, recognized their sinful ways, and turned to God.

When we accept Jesus's invitation to salvation, it means much more than the promise of heaven. Do not misunderstand; heaven is terrific and will be an immense blessing in the future. But salvation also gives us a new life on Earth. We leave our old life behind. We no longer operate independently of God, doing our own thing our way. When we enter a meaningful relationship with God, we enter his kingdom and begin doing things God's way.

The apostle Paul instructed the new and growing church to put off the habits of their former lives. "Therefore, if anyone is in Christ, he is a new creation. The old has passed away; behold, the new has come" (2 Corinthians 5:17 ESV). The Bible also promises blessings for all people who walk in God's ways. "Blessed is everyone who fears the Lord, who walks in his ways!" (Psalm 128:1 ESV).

To walk in God's ways means "to live or behave in a specific manner."[26] What we believe about God and our relationship with him will influence our behavior. We will trust God to the point that we give up doing things our way and embrace his perspective, desire, and agenda for life. In God's eyes, every person has value and is worthy of love and respect. He longs for us to walk in a loving relationship with him. His agenda is that one day, everything here on Earth will be just like it is in heaven.

God's way of life radically differs from anything we experience on Earth, where selfishness often prevails. We want to enjoy life and experience all the good things. Our me-first attitude means we tend to prioritize our own needs at the expense of those around us. And the more we have, the more we want, and we don't like being told no.

Our selfish attitude can color how we view God. We often have the misconception that God is a cosmic killjoy and that his commandments are a way to take away all pleasure and enjoyment from life. But nothing could be further from the truth. God's ways are designed to produce a way of life that is mutually beneficial for all who dwell under his rule. Remember who God is and his character: He always wants what is best for us.

The blessing that is promised is twofold. God does reward our obedience, and if we follow him, we can expect his favor. But there is also a blessing that naturally flows from each of God's commands. This is because God's ways are designed to enhance life, making our existence much more enjoyable for everyone who dwells within his kingdom.

In our sin-infested world, we are not doing such a good job of treating others well. Too often, we want to blame our sad state on God, but it is based on our choices and actions.

God makes it clear how he expects us to live. In his Word, he lays out his blueprint for living in a way that ensures we will have a positive influence on the world around us. We see this blueprint in the Ten Commandments (see Exodus 20:1-17 and Deuteronomy 5:6-21). Interestingly, most of these commandments outline how we should treat one another, and most people agree, at least in part, with these principles. We are comfortable with the idea that we should not take what doesn't belong to us, we should tell the truth, we are to listen to our parents, and killing another person is wrong. These are things we are taught as children. We may not always follow them, but for the most part, we believe these laws are the right thing to do, and we are comfortable with them.

However, many of God's instructions push us out of our comfort zones. We balk at the idea of following them because we question their wisdom. They seem to contradict our nature and personal life experiences. We have an ingrained survival instinct and naturally want to protect ourselves and those we love. We fear that obeying these ideals will lead to our demise. As a result, God's commands stretch our faith as we learn to trust him and his ways. Let's take a look at some of Jesus's "out of our comfort zone" teachings.

The Sermon on the Mount

The Sermon on the Mount, chronicled in Matthew chapters 5–7, was revolutionary when Jesus delivered it to a hungry audience. Today, his words are still life-changing if we are willing to follow them. They are a key part of God's plan.

The essence of the Sermon on the Mount's radical principles is this: How we treat others matters. God tells us to treat one another with love, kindness, and respect. Our behavior influences how they feel about themselves and impacts how we view ourselves. What does it say about us if we are people with contempt, divisiveness, malice, and disrespect? Is that the type of person we can be proud to be? Our culture often admires the ruthless, power-hungry person who pursues their goals and steps on anyone who stands in their way. While we might envy their accomplishments, is this someone we would like as a best friend or neighbor? How would we ever be comfortable with them, knowing that they would stab us in the back just to meet their selfish desires? The bottom line is that character matters. God's ways are designed to produce and develop people of strong, righteous character who treat others the way they should be treated.

> Do not let any unwholesome talk come out of your mouths, but only what is helpful for building others up according to their needs, that it may benefit those who listen. And do not grieve the Holy Spirit of God, with whom you were sealed for the day of redemption. Get rid of all bitterness, rage and anger, brawling and slander, along with every form of malice. Be kind and compassionate to one another, forgiving each other, just as in Christ God forgave you (Ephesians 4:29–32).

As we read through the Sermon on the Mount, we may feel, "I can't do that; it's impossible to live that way!" Here's the good news: That is the point of the entire sermon. On our own, we are incapable of living in such a manner; we don't have it in us. But when we walk in a close relationship with God and allow him to work in our lives, we will treat others the way God asks.

The Golden Rule

Most of us are familiar with the Golden Rule: "Treat others just as you want to be treated" (Luke 6:31 CEV). At first glance, this is wisdom we can accept. It makes sense. We like to be treated with respect and kindness, so we should treat others in the same manner. It is an uplifting ideology, and we feel good about ourselves when we follow it.

This principle is easy to apply to others who are generally kind, loving, and good to us. However, it is a different story when we need to deal with people who are mean, disrespectful, and generally difficult to work with. But God does not say that we are off the hook if someone treats us poorly. We are still held accountable for treating them with love, kindness, and respect.

In this context, the Golden Rule is hard to swallow. Often, we are mirrors of those we surround ourselves with. We tend to be the same way if we are around uplifting, positive people. It is as if they bring out the best in us, and we are a better version of ourselves. Unfortunately, the same is true for the other side of the coin. Negative, unkind, and unloving people bring out the worst in us. When we are around difficult people, our Golden Rule is twisted into this: "Treat others the way they treat us," and we adopt similar behavior. That is why God gave us the difficult task of loving our enemies.

Loving Our Enemies

The Bible clearly defines how we are to deal with those who treat us poorly. "Love your enemies! Do good to them. Lend to them without expecting to be repaid. Then your reward from heaven will be very great, and you will truly be acting as children of the Most High, for he is kind to those who are unthankful and wicked" (Luke 6:35 NLT).

Loving our enemies is essential to dealing effectively with difficult people. We want to model our actions after God's ways. This verse shows us that God is kind to the ungrateful and the wicked. That does not mean that God does not discipline them for their inappropriate behavior or that he will not withhold his favor for their bad behavior. What it does mean is that he is not mean and vindictive. God does not change his character; he will always be kind and loving, even toward those who do not deserve it. The point of this verse is that we are also undeserving of God's kindness. We are all fallen human beings, and we live by our sinful nature. It is only by the grace of God that we are where we are. In turn, we must always keep God's grace as our focus when dealing with difficult people.

Another point in this verse is that we must never change our character or who we are to accommodate negative people. Take a good look at who they are. They are mean, angry, jealous, and spiteful. Is that the person you want to become? I believe there are negative role models. Some people live in such disarray that we know we never want to be like them. Still, God encourages us to maintain our godly character by treating others with kindness and respect. That is how God responds, and we should follow his example. Ultimately, we will feel better about ourselves when we take God's high road.

Loving an enemy might mean that we need to confront them about their behavior. However, as we challenge them, we must do so with kindness and respect. Our goal should be to help this person understand how their behavior hurts them and those around them, and to enable them to change their ways. A fundamental spiritual truth is that we cannot effect positive change through negative behavior. Positive change begins with love, kindness, and respect. Love conquers all!

We are always responsible for loving our enemies. There is a possibility that, despite all our efforts to love them, they may never appear to change. Only God can change hearts. Every person is held accountable for their decisions. And because God has given us free will, he will never force us to change. He can do everything in his power to influence us, but he will never override the freedom he has given us. God can use you to help this person. We may never know the impact we have. Where there is love, there is hope.

Forgiveness

God's command to love our enemies also reveals an essential but complex spiritual discipline: forgiveness. I must admit that forgiving someone for the wrong they have inflicted on me is often a raw and painful experience. It seems unfair, and I want to shout to God, "But don't you care about what they did to me?"

There are three main reasons why forgiveness is the most difficult of God's commands. First, it means that something terrible has happened that we cannot get past. We feel deeply wounded, and God's instruction doesn't seem fair. In many ways, asking us to forgive someone goes against our instinct. Self-preservation is a fundamental aspect of human nature, essential for protecting us from harm. No rational person will purposely put themselves in physical danger. This also extends to emotional damage. And we should defend ourselves.

The second reason we find forgiveness so painful is that we desire justice. If someone hurts us, we want them to be held accountable for their actions. Unfortunately, in our pain, our form of justice becomes distorted. We want to exact revenge on that person and compensation for the pain they caused us, and we try to make things fair by seeking justice. However, revenge is a sin and will only worsen the situation. We might find temporary satisfaction in payback, but it does not make the initial situation disappear. The pain and hurt are still there. However, the problem will now escalate into further retaliation.

Third, forgiveness is challenging due to misconceptions about its meaning. Our faulty understanding closes our minds to all that actual forgiveness has to offer. Too often, we are reluctant to forgive someone because we don't fully understand what true forgiveness means.

The good news is that God does not expect us to follow his commands on our own. He knows our human weaknesses and our limited human abilities. True forgiveness is only possible if one has a solid relationship with God. His ways might go against every fiber of our being, but we can rely on his character and admit that we do not have the best solution.

Once we understand why forgiveness is such a struggle, we can take the following steps to forgive. First, we must realize that God knows the offense; nothing is hidden from his sight. This can make the situation more difficult because we question why God did not stop it from happening. However, we may never know why, and we must learn to trust that God has his reasons. He feels your hurt and pain, and he cares deeply about you.

Next, we must recognize that forgiveness does not mean that what happened is okay. We are not expected to turn to that person and say, "It's okay that you hurt me; it's no big deal." But God wants us to give that pain to him. In the Psalms, King David writes about his struggles with his enemies, and he pens these words of comfort: "You keep track of all my sorrows. You have collected all my tears in your bottle. You have recorded each one in your book" (Psalm 56:8 NLT). You can be assured that God does the same for you.

The final step is to prayerfully turn the entire situation over to God, knowing that he will handle it in his timing and in his way. Even when it seems the other person has gotten away with hurting you, there is no such thing in God's kingdom because there is always a negative consequence for sin. God detests sin, and we have his assurance that he will not leave the guilty unpunished. He will, however, do it in a manner that is just and fair.

Forgiveness is an imperative that stretches us. I won't lie; I often want to ignore this command and handle things my way. However, life experience has taught me that my way is not the best. I can honestly say that I have never regretted doing things God's way. While forgiveness is hard, we have the assurance that God will be our champion as we trust him and follow his ways. He always wants what is best for us and will do everything in his power to see it happen. We will experience God's healing touch as he comforts us in our pain and attends to our wounds. The Bible tells us that God is close to the brokenhearted and will be with us during difficult times. We can also be confident that God will do what is just and make things right. God declares, "Revenge is mine!" (Romans 12:9 NIV). Woe to him who is in the path of God's revenge.

When we choose to do things God's way and forgive, an amazing thing happens. We find that we are free from all the negativity of the awful situation and can move past it. We are no longer victims and will become people of strength, courage, and character.

As for Rick and Marty, I hope that one day they find that treasure and that it is everything they hoped for. It would be so exciting to see the mystery finally solved and the treasure revealed. All their hard work and persistence will finally have paid off as they unveil what has been hidden for centuries. But there is the reality that they may never find it, and we will never know what happened to it, and the deep mysteries will remain unsolved. Thankfully, the treasure in God's kingdom can be found by walking in a meaningful relationship with him. We will become the best version of ourselves as we learn to live the way God wants. As we learn to love, respect, and forgive others we will be blessed with positive relationships. We will enjoy peace, joy, and contentment, and our lives will be full of God's goodness. And that is a treasure that is beyond compare.

PART 2

Why Should I Listen to Him?

CHAPTER 5

What's in It for Me?

What are the benefits of living in a relationship with God, and why should we listen to him? The benefits are filled with blessings, joy, and hope for the future. Jesus tells us that he came so that we might have life "more abundantly" (John 10:10 NKJV). In the second part of this book, we will explore this gloriously abundant life. This chapter will focus on what we can expect from our relationship with God.

One thing to know about me is that I love dogs. It doesn't matter what breed, size, or color; I love them all. My family has always had dogs, and I don't know what life is like without one. The relationship between dogs and humans is so special, and it is incredible what dogs are willing to do for us.

Thirty years ago, I discovered canine agility and was hooked. It has become a rewarding hobby, and I compete regularly with two dogs, Buzz and Rex, who are adorable Cavalier King Charles Spaniels. Agility tests the bond between a dog and its handler as the team navigates an obstacle course. The goal is to complete the course correctly within a specific time. It is a sport requiring teamwork. The dog must learn particular behaviors to complete each obstacle correctly. Each obstacle presents its challenge, as the dogs must navigate jumps, tunnels, upright poles, and narrow planks. They must also learn to listen to their handlers' instructions while navigating the course. It is fascinating to watch handlers and dogs work harmoniously to complete a challenging course.

I have learned a great deal over the years, primarily through teaching these complex behaviors. It requires tremendous patience and motivation from both the dog and the handler. I have developed two key dog training rules that are essential to a great partnership.

The first rule is that a trainer must realize that dogs are primarily motivated by what is in it for them. A dog needs to get some benefit or reward for their actions. My second rule is that a trainer can never force a dog to do something; we must make the dog want to do it. No amount of force or yelling will make a dog do something it does not want to do. The best approach is to allow the dog to think this behavior is their idea. The wise trainer will allow the dog to make the choices and reward the correct behavior. These two rules are tied together, and a good trainer will discover what motivates their dog. The goal is to reward the dog and to make training fun for them. A dog will quickly associate this positive experience with training and love the sport. A happy dog is engaged with its handler and is enthusiastic about working. I have seen many dogs dragging their handler toward the agility ring in their desire to perform.

There is a spiritual analogy to my dog training rules. While we are complex, intelligent beings, in some ways, we are no different than man's best friend. Deep within our souls, we want to know, "What's in it for me?" Before we commit to a task, we want to know what we will gain from it. To some, this may sound selfish and indulgent. There is the false idea that, as Christians, we should not be concerned about our desires and hopes. We need to set aside our self-concern and prioritize God and others. It's true that God does want us to love him, and he asks us to care for others. But he does not want us to deny who we are to the point that we are doormats. God does not expect us to serve him without benefit. What kind of relationship would that be if we gave and gave but never received anything in return? It would be a dysfunctional, unhealthy relationship. If that were the case, who would want to be in a relationship in the first place?

The simple truth is that God is all about us. He created us, loves us, thinks about us, provides for us, and plans for our future. One of the major themes of Psalms is how much God cares for us. Psalm 139 in the New Living Translation (NLT) is one of my favorites. It illustrates God's intimate involvement in our lives. Take a moment to consider these beautiful verses taken from that chapter.

O Lord, you have examined my heart and know everything about me. You know when I sit down or stand up. You know my thoughts even when I'm far away. You see me when I travel and when I rest at home. You know everything I do (vv. 1–3).

I can never escape from your Spirit! I can never get away from your presence! If I go up to heaven, you are there; if I go down to the grave, you are there. If I ride the wings of the morning, if I dwell by the farthest oceans, even there your hand will guide me, and your strength will support me (vv. 7–10).

You saw me before I was born. Every day of my life was recorded in your book. Every moment was laid out before a single day had passed (v. 16).

How precious are your thoughts about me, O God. They cannot be numbered! I can't even count them; they outnumber the grains of sand! And when I wake up, you are still with me! (vv. 17–18).

God's love and concern have nothing to do with who we are and whether we are worthy to receive that love. It is all about who God is. Love forms the foundation of God's character, and everything he says and does is motivated by love. This love goes way beyond warm, fuzzy feelings. It is deep, personal, and willing to go the extra mile. God is our champion. He is unequivocally on our side, as he actively works for us and always has our best interests in mind. "So what should we say about this? If God is with us, no one can defeat us" (Romans 8:31 NCV).

Since God is our champion, there are numerous benefits to living in a relationship with him. Let's take a look at some of them so we can fully understand what is in it for us as we walk in a relationship with God.

The first benefit is discovering the purpose and meaning of our lives. Most people, at some point, question their life's purpose. We all want to know what our life is all about. Is it more than just the job we perform, the things we do, or our family? We long to know where we come from, why we are here, and where we are going. However, those questions often remain unanswered, leaving us confused and hopeless. To find our purpose in life, we must begin with God, our Creator.

It is essential to recognize that God never creates anything without a purpose. The sky, the oceans, dry land, animals, and the smallest living organisms all serve a purpose in the world. There are no accidents or mistakes in God's eyes. "Long before he laid Earth's foundations, he had us in mind, had settled on us as the focus of his love, to be made whole and holy by his love. Long, long ago he decided to adopt us into his family through Jesus Christ" (Ephesians 1:4 MSG).

Pastor and author Rick Warren tells us that "you were made by God and you were made for God. Until you understand that your life will never make any sense."[27]

The first step in finding our life's purpose is understanding this simple truth: God's purpose is rooted in his love for us and his desire to be in relationship with us. It is the reason why we were created. As we understand who God is, we learn to trust him and embrace his plan for our lives. We will not reach that point until we begin walking daily with him. We have free will, and knowing God's plan is not enough. We must willingly do as he asks.

God's plan for our lives helps to ground us. When we walk with him, we are no longer caught in the cycle of looking for that "something" that makes sense, only to find that it adds to our confusion. Your something might be a successful career, finding your soulmate, or establishing a healthy bank account. But all these are fleeting and can be taken away in a heartbeat. They are worthy goals, but they can never give us our purpose. We find our purpose only in God.

Life becomes meaningful when it is aligned with God's purpose. He uses everything that happens to help us grow and mature. Even our dark times are part of God's plan and purpose. While they might be painful and difficult, God will use them to do something good in our lives. I have faced many difficult periods in my life, and God has always been there to guide me through them. Looking back, I can see how his hand was guiding every circumstance. When I faced uncertainty and confusion, he brought clarity. At times, I rebelled, and the results of that rebellion were not pretty because God needed to correct me. I admit I made stupid choices, but I learned from them. I am grateful for God's purpose because I know myself well enough that I would have made a complete mess of my life on my own.

God's purpose has two parts. The first includes all of humanity. "For God so loved the world that he gave his one and only Son, that whoever believes in him shall not perish but have eternal life" (John 3:16). The invitation to have a relationship with him is open to everyone. God's blessings are for anyone who believes in his promises and follows his will.

The second part of God's purpose is for the individual. "And we know that for those who love God all things work together for good, for those who are called according to his purpose" (Romans 8:28 ESV). God has a plan for each of us, a plan tailored to our unique personalities and talents. He wants every individual to participate actively in his work here on Earth. He longs for us to experience the joy of helping to change lives. We all bear the responsibility to positively touch others and help them understand who God is. I cannot stress this enough: How we treat others matters! We can build people up and improve their lives, or we can tear them down and hurt them.

Another benefit of having a relationship with God is that he has provided his unlimited resources to help us be a positive influence on others. We do not have to do it on our own. In utilizing these resources, we will thrive and enjoy an exciting, fulfilling life. The Bible gives the analogy of a root system to describe how life looks when we are connected to God. "That person is like a tree planted by streams of water, which yields its fruit in season and whose leaf does not wither—whatever they do prospers" (Psalm 1:3).

We saw this earlier when we looked at the vine and its branches. Similar analogies are given throughout the Bible that describe our "spiritual root system." We cannot nourish and support ourselves. We need to be rooted in Christ and draw upon his spiritual power. As we saw earlier, we remain rooted in Christ through reading the Bible, prayer, and fellowship with other believers.[28]

The apostle Peter outlined how we can serve others in 1 Peter 4:10, "Each of you should use whatever gift you have received to serve others, as faithful stewards of God's grace in its various forms." Access to God's resources is a blessing to his children. They enable us to become people of good moral character, and this blessing enhances our lives. But it is also important to consider that God blesses us so that we can be a blessing to others.[29]

One of the resources we can tap into is God's perfect and unconditional love. There is nothing we can do that would cause him to stop loving us. God's love is faithful, meaning it will endure throughout all eternity. He promises to love us, and he keeps his vows. His passion always seeks our best interest. Even his discipline is done out of love. He will correct us and lead us in the right direction so that we do not harm ourselves.

Through God's perfect love, we learn to love ourselves. We begin to understand our value and worth as we learn to appreciate how God created us. First John 4:16 says, "So we have come to know and to believe the love that God has for us. God is love, and whoever abides in love abides in God, and God abides in him" (ESV).

As our self-worth grows, we begin to see others in a new light. We begin to value them, and the love God has shown us overflows from our being onto those around us. As a result, our relationships will thrive and flourish. We will become better spouses and better parents. We will have a better connection with our coworkers and friends.

A good illustration of how we can learn to love others is the parable of the Good Samaritan told by Jesus in Luke 10:30–37.

> Jesus said: "A man was going down from Jerusalem to Jericho, when he was attacked by robbers. They stripped him of his clothes, beat him and went away, leaving him half dead. A priest happened to be going down the same road, and when he saw the man, he passed by on the other side. So too, a Levite, when he came to the place and saw him, passed by on the other side. But a Samaritan, as he traveled, came where the man was; and when he saw him, he took pity on him. He went to him and bandaged his wounds, pouring on oil and wine. Then he put the man on his own donkey, brought him to an inn and took care of him. The next day he took out two denarii and gave them to the innkeeper. 'Look after him,' he said, 'and when I return, I will reimburse you for any extra expense you may have.'"

This parable emphasizes the importance of showing compassion and love to others. We do not know much about the man who was attacked, except that he was most likely a Jew. His Jewish brothers, the priest and the Levite, chose to ignore God's command to love their neighbor and left this man on the side of the road. On the other hand, a Samaritan, who is considered an enemy to the Jews, stopped to help the man. Out of compassion and love, this Samaritan was willing to cross cultural barriers to come to the aid of the injured man. This parable challenges personal biases and emphasizes that everyone is worthy of compassion and love, regardless of their background. The way that we show this kind of love to others is by emulating the love that God has shown to us.

Another vital resource that we receive from God is wisdom. Wisdom is crucial for making informed decisions that lead to positive outcomes. It applies knowledge and uses discernment in decision-making, and it is a vital ingredient for a meaningful life. If we lack wisdom, all we need to do is ask God. James 1:5 promises, "If any of you lacks wisdom, let him ask God, who gives generously to all without reproach, and it will be given him" (ESV).

Why is God's wisdom so important? To make solid choices, we need to apply knowledge to the situation. We often lack enough information to form a complete picture. On the other hand, God knows everything; nothing is hidden from him. When we ask him for wisdom, he will often reveal essential details that we need to consider.

We also need discernment to help us filter through all the available information and select what is relevant and accurate to our situation. Today, the truth is becoming increasingly difficult to find. We all know that just because a statement appears online, it does not necessarily mean it's true. Even if the author has a persuasive argument, does that prove they're right?

This is when we should ask God for wisdom. God is truth; it is part of his nature, which means he can never lie or try to deceive. He is honest and always wants what is best.

He is not motivated by greed or selfishness because that is not part of his nature. God's motivation is always love. John 17:17 affirms that we can trust God's words. It says, "Sanctify them in the truth; your word is truth" (ESV).

To help us discern truth, God gave us his Holy Spirit. The Holy Spirit will teach us right from wrong and will help us discern the truth from a lie. "But the Helper, the Holy Spirit, whom the Father will send in My name, He will teach you all things, and bring to your remembrance all things that I said to you" (John 14:26 NKJV).

Next, we engage our minds. He will give us knowledge and help us discern the truth, but he does not choose for us. He wants us to use the tools he has given us to make our decisions. In giving us free will, he shows us that he does not want robots. He wants intelligent children who learn to make wise choices as they listen to him.

Another resource we can tap into is God's peace. It is unlike worldly peace, which is fleeting. God's peace endures despite our Earthly circumstances, providing harmony and calmness to our entire being. "You will keep in perfect peace all who trust in you, all whose thoughts are fixed on you!" (Isaiah 26:3 NLT).

Let's be honest. We live in a chaotic world filled with anxiety. Anxiety is our body's response to stress, uncertainty, and perceived danger. While anxiety in small doses can be a natural and even helpful response, persistent or intense anxiety can become overwhelming and isolating. This commonly useful emotion becomes a problem when it begins to interfere with daily life, relationships, or overall well-being.

God's peace is the antidote for our anxiety. The type of peace God gives can be described as *shalom*. Shalom has a deep and multifaceted meaning. The Hebrew word "shalom" carries an expansive meaning that includes peace, completeness, wholeness, well-being, and harmony. Rather than signifying only the absence of war or conflict, it reflects a holistic state of flourishing in every aspect of life—relational, physical, familial, and spiritual.[30] It involves a quietness of heart within us, spiritual health and prosperity, the adequacy to meet life's demands, and the kind of spiritual well-being that transcends circumstances. We have the privilege of laying our burdens before God in prayer, knowing that he will listen and respond. When we live in a relationship with God, we are never alone. He is always with us and is ready to respond to our needs. This relieves us of the burden of feeling solely responsible for outcomes, easing anxious thoughts.

Another resource from God is hope. Hope is that spark—the belief that things can get better, that there's light ahead even in dark times. It's what keeps people moving forward, even when obstacles pile up. Some see hope as an emotion, others as a mindset, and still others as a source of strength. It is found in everyday moments, in dreams, in resilience, and in the quiet understanding that change is always possible. When we put our hope in God, we have this marvelous promise: "'For I know what I have planned for you,' says the Lord. 'I have plans to prosper you, not to harm you. I have plans to give you a future filled with hope'" (Jeremiah 29:11 NET).

Our hope is based on who God is and on what he has done in the past. We have the assurance that he will continue to do the same in the future. This hope enables us to maintain a positive attitude and mindset even in the darkest times. Hope helps us acknowledge our problems and address them, knowing that through God's guidance, we will ultimately achieve victory. This powerful motivator propels us forward and helps us envision a better future. We all could use a good dose of God's hope!

Your life will be more fulfilling when you have a relationship with your Creator. God breathed his life into you. He knows your purpose and what you can accomplish. With God, you will go further than you can relying solely on your own ability or talent. To fully understand the boundless benefits of this relationship, you must experience them for yourself—and God has much to offer you!

CHAPTER 6

Tale of an Ugly Table

Many years ago, I moved into my first apartment. I was fresh out of college, funds were tight, and trying to furnish my new apartment on a limited budget was a bit challenging. Luckily, I had a friend who knew of my situation and offered her help. She was moving out of a house that she shared with friends and had found several pieces of unwanted furniture. Knowing I needed furniture, she invited me over to take a look.

There were reasons why this furniture was undesirable, but I recognized that "beggars can't be choosers," and free was a hard price to beat. So, I met my friend at the house, and we went through each room, picking out pieces I thought I could use. Eventually, we went down the stairs to the basement, where I immediately spotted the most hideous table I had ever seen tucked in a corner. It was covered in dust, grime, and layers of peeling paint, the most recent being a bright yellow. As I approached for a closer look, I saw rings on the top where oil or some other substance had leaked. Needless to say, the table looked very sad. However, it was the perfect size, and my practical friend advised that no one would know what was underneath if I covered it with a tablecloth.

So, I heeded my friend's advice and took the table home to my apartment. I cleaned it up, found a nice flowery tablecloth to cover it, and tucked it in the corner of my kitchen where it wouldn't draw too much attention. I called it my "wallflower table." Although it was the most unsightly piece of furniture, I had to admit it was sturdy and functional. It was a great place to drop groceries when coming home from the store. I spent many mornings eating breakfast and having my morning devotions at that table. There were even a few romantic dinners (with a lovely new tablecloth) held there with my future husband.

When the time came to move out of my apartment, I was torn about what to do with the functional but oh-so-ugly table. Maybe it was time to get rid of it. While we debated what to do, my fiancé took off the tablecloth to take a better look at the wood. Using his penknife, he scraped off some of the layers of accumulated paint. There, under years of paint, he found maple wood. Maple is a desirable hardwood for furniture because it is very durable. It is also gorgeous when stained, bringing out the rich color and wood grain. My fiancé advised me to clean it up and keep it because "they just don't make beautiful furniture like this anymore!"

So, I took the table out to the garage and began the tedious task of stripping off all the old paint. Sure enough, beneath all the paint was the most beautiful tabletop. I pried the top apart and found a tooth and gear mechanism for a leaf. Even better! I was excited. A bigger table would be more valuable. As I continued the restoration, I discovered some interesting details that I had never noticed before.

On the underside of one end of the table were indents made many years before with a pencil. I could imagine a boy sitting there doing his homework. In his frustration or boredom, he poked his pencil into the table, leaving marks. Not only was my table now beautiful, but it also had a nostalgic charm.

I found a few chairs to match my newfound table, and it became the centerpiece of my dining room. I no longer covered it with a tablecloth because I did not want to cover up its beauty and character. I no longer kept it hidden because I wanted everyone who came to my house to notice and hear its story. Many years have passed, and I still have that table.

I learned an important lesson from my old table: It takes a wise person to recognize the value of what appears to be a piece of junk. I would have thrown it out if my husband had not told me that the ugly table was made of valuable maple. Once I understood its value, I was willing to do the work to restore it.

God sees us the same way. Despite our appearance, he knows our value and will pour himself into restoring us if we allow him to do so. "Are not five sparrows sold for two pennies? And not one of them is forgotten before God. Why, even the hairs of your head are all numbered. Fear not; you are of more value than many sparrows" (Luke 12:6–7 ESV).

I love these verses. They illustrate God's tender care even of the smallest creature. When I think about sparrows, it is easy to dismiss them as disposable and insignificant. Yet my world would seem empty without their cheerful song. God created these songbirds for a purpose, and he values each of them. Not one of them perishes without God noticing.

These verses also show us that this same tender care is extended to us, his most special creation. Think about it: The hairs on our heads are numbered! Talk about attention to detail. Down to the smallest features, God values us. He is always with us, and we are always on his mind. "How precious to me are your thoughts, O God! How vast is the sum of them! If I would count them, they are more than the sand. I awake, and I am still with you" (Psalm 139:17–18 ESV).

The idea that God is always thinking about me and making plans for my future makes me feel valued. I matter to him. And the same is true for every one of God's children. We are all his favorites. It reminds me of a dear friend of mine, a wise and godly woman. She had several grandchildren, and she used her golden years to instill value in each of them. She did many fun things with them, and she made a point to spend quality one-on-one time with each of them. When she passed away, and as the grandchildren gathered, one of them proclaimed, "I was her favorite." Another chimed in, "No, I was her favorite." The grandchildren came to realize that they all felt they were her favorite. How blessed these grandchildren were, knowing that they were valued and loved. This woman's legacy beautifully illustrates how God treats us.

God wants us to understand our value and how much he cares for us. He then wants us to use that truth to shape our self-view. People sometimes evaluate their worth based on external factors or circumstances that are beyond their control. They may compare themselves to others using these standards. This approach can be problematic, as differences in appearance, intelligence, or financial status are common. Such comparisons may contribute to feelings of inadequacy.

This standard is not only superficial but also temporary. Our looks will fade with time. One day, our minds will not be as sharp. Money gets spent and can quickly run out. Fame and power can run dry, leaving us empty. Like my table, we become covered in life's troubles and realize we don't like what we've become.

When we use superficial standards to determine our value, we put the cart before the horse and go nowhere. We can turn the cart around when we recognize that, in God's eyes, we already have value no matter who we are, how we look, or what we do. We were born with that value. If we accept God's evaluation of us, we will move on to value ourselves. If we reject God's appraisal, we will continue to use false standards to evaluate ourselves and will never fully understand and appreciate our true worth.

Out of love, God gave his precious Son to redeem us back to himself. The Gospel of John tells us, "For God so loved the world that He gave his only Son. Whoever puts his trust in God's Son will not be lost but will have life that lasts forever" (John 3:16 NLV).

Our human minds can only begin to imagine this level of sacrifice. He sent his Son away, and as a result, they lost the close relationship they had enjoyed. Being God, Jesus had it all: status, power, knowledge, and authority. Yet he gave up everything to humbly come to Earth to be among us. Meditate on this for a moment. God laid everything he treasured on the line to save you and me. Jesus illustrates his love for us in Luke 15:3–5: "If you had a hundred sheep and one of them strayed away and was lost in the wilderness, wouldn't you leave the ninety-nine others to go and search for the lost one until you found it? And then you would joyfully carry it home on your shoulders" (TLB).

I once saw a painting that struck a chord about how much Jesus cares for me. It was a picture of Jesus running through the muddy, wet woods chasing a lost lamb while the entire flock watched in the distance. This image conveys the profound understanding that Jesus is willing to leave all behind to pursue us when we wander, and he brings us back home where we belong.

God's evident willingness to go to great lengths to rescue us shows how much he values us. Why are we so important to God, and why was he willing to give up so much to rescue us? Our value is found in God's desire for family, and each member is vital to him. He designed us as distinct individuals with great intention and purpose. In the Psalms, David ponders how God individually designs each of us. "You watched me as I was being formed in utter seclusion, as I was woven together in the dark of the womb. You saw me before I was born. Every day of my life was recorded in your book. Every moment was laid out before a single day had passed" (Psalm 139:15–16 NLT).

These verses reveal much about God's character. In his eyes, there are no accidents, mistakes, or worthless people. He made us with value, and it is an innate part of who we are. It's up to us as to what we do with that fact. Remember, out of great love, God also gave us the freedom to choose. We can accept his valuation of our being or continue to evaluate ourselves based on superficial standards.

God continues to show us our value by how he treats us. He loves us unconditionally. No matter how much we mess up, God will still love us. Our mistakes do not cause us to lose value because God offers us forgiveness. Forgiveness is based on what Jesus Christ did on the cross when he paid the penalty for our sins. It is not based on our merit or worthiness. No matter what we do, we cannot make up for our wrongdoing. God's forgiveness cannot be earned; it is his gift to us. "Therefore, my friends, I want you to know that through Jesus the forgiveness of sins is proclaimed to you" (Acts 13:38).

Forgiveness is available to all who wish to take it and are willing to confess their wrongdoings. We do not have to worry about being good enough or worthy of it. God created us with value, and we can choose his forgiveness freely.

God also proves our value by his willingness to invest in our lives. He loves us for who we are right now. But he also values who we will become as he invests himself in our futures. We will discuss the transformation process in Chapter 7. God knows our potential and will work diligently to help us reach it. He is our champion, constantly working to bring out the best in us. The process is sometimes painful and challenging, but we can be assured that God is always working in our best interests.

Through our relationship with God, we begin to understand our value, and we should use that understanding to shape our identity. Through this relationship, in which we are valued and loved, we become the people we are meant to be. We need to learn how to love ourselves.

We already discussed the verse below earlier, but let's examine it further. It reveals an important natural progression worth noting.

> Hearing that Jesus had silenced the Sadducees, the Pharisees got together. One of them, an expert in the law, tested him with this question: "Teacher, which is the greatest commandment in the Law?" Jesus replied: "'Love the Lord your God with all your heart and with all your soul and with all your mind.' This is the first and greatest commandment. And the second is like it: 'Love your neighbor as yourself'" (Matthew 22:34–39).

If I have learned one thing through the years, it is that there is always a balance to God's way of doing things. This verse shows us that the balance cannot be maintained until we first learn to love God with all our being. When we walk in harmony with him, we will begin to understand our value in his eyes and receive his love. We will learn to accept his forgiveness and recognize that God sees us as a work in progress. Looking at the beautiful world around us, we can see that God does not make junk. His work in our lives will always produce something exquisite and attractive. Then, as we grow in our relationship with him, our hearts will overflow, and we will love others in the way they deserve to be loved.

So, how do we learn to value ourselves and love who we are? First, we change our mental attitude. Deep down, many of us are uncomfortable loving ourselves—and saying it out loud isn't socially acceptable. If we walk around proclaiming that we love ourselves, we can easily be labeled as narcissists, self-absorbed, or selfish. However, there is a significant distinction between being self-absorbed and genuinely loving oneself. A self-absorbed person is generally insecure about their identity and constantly needs reassurance and approval. People who understand their value and have learned to love themselves can give back to others because they are secure in their own identity.

The second way we can value ourselves is to stop looking at others to determine our worth. We habitually compare ourselves to others, deriving our self-worth from how well we measure up. But this only denies us the opportunity to be unique individuals. If we always try to be like someone else, we will never become who we are meant to be. In his letter to the Galatian church, the apostle Paul encouraged them to "pay careful attention to your own work, for then you will get the satisfaction of a job well done, and you won't need to compare yourself to anyone else" (Galatians 6:4 NLT).

Finally, we value ourselves by stopping self-judgment. Do you find that you inwardly criticize and judge yourself repeatedly? We are often our own worst critics. We focus so much on what is wrong that we can't see the good. Getting hung up on things we can't change leaves little room for self-acceptance. God doesn't expect perfection from us. He is fully aware of our flaws and imperfections and still loves us unconditionally as we are. He will never reject us for our faults because he intends to turn our weaknesses into strengths. This is the beauty of God's transforming power.

We love ourselves when we support our well-being, which means taking care of the physical body that God has given us. We need to make sure we are eating right, taking time to exercise, and getting enough sleep. We also love ourselves by taking care of our mental health. We can do this by limiting stress. We need to learn to take a break from our daily grind to do something we enjoy, even if it is to take a nap. We must tend to our spiritual health by spending time in God's Word and prayer. Our well-being should be a priority. We do not take care of others at the expense of ourselves. Instead, we take care of others by first taking care of ourselves.

We also love ourselves by recognizing our failures and mistakes. That means we need to stop having unrealistic expectations of who we are. We must accept that we are not perfect but love a perfect God. When we do, our failures become teachable moments to help us grow and mature. Our shortcomings should not be viewed as an attack on our self-worth. We can freely acknowledge our faults, knowing that God is at work to strengthen us and make us a better version of ourselves.

As we learn to love ourselves, we start to see life in a different light. Our new perspective will influence how we interact with others. When we acknowledge that God values us, we will come to understand that all people have inherent value. When we receive God's forgiveness, we are better equipped to forgive others. We must treat others as God does, with respect and unconditional love.

We have reached a point where learning to love ourselves is essential for thriving. As sin grows and evil flourishes, human life is devalued. We view the homeless, the addict, and the mentally ill as social problems, and we no longer see them as human beings with value. We put those who make videos of themselves doing ridiculous things on a pedestal; yet we often overlook those who make positive contributions. Social media is no longer a place to connect with your friends and family and have fun. It has evolved into a platform for criticizing, bullying, demeaning, and disrespecting others. It has become a constant battle to maintain our self-worth.

There will always be those who try to diminish your value. Don't listen to them and never forget your value in God's eyes. The lesson from my table is that our Creator treasures you and me. He knows our great worth. And his is the only view that matters.

CHAPTER 7

Wind to Fill My Sails

A few summers ago, my husband and I vacationed in Annapolis, Maryland. Annapolis is located on Chesapeake Bay and claims to be the sailing capital of the world. It is no wonder, considering the size of the Bay and the endless miles of coves and inlets to explore. There are sailboats everywhere you look.

At the time of our visit to Annapolis, a large sailing regatta was scheduled to take place. I knew nothing about sailing, so this was an excellent opportunity to watch and learn. Early that weekend, the sailors began to arrive in full force. I watched with great interest as sailboat after sailboat was lifted from its trailer and carefully placed in the water. As the sailing crews arrived to check on their boats, the docks were abuzz with activity. The hulls were checked for any damage and to make sure no dirt or debris could slow the boats' performances. The decks were washed and scrubbed clean. All the lines and rigging were checked to ensure everything was in order. The sails were hoisted, inspected, and carefully packed away for the big event.

The next morning, the sailors arrived early to begin the race preparations. Strategies were planned over steaming cups of coffee. Every fine detail was discussed, down to the clothing the crew would wear. Navigation charts were consulted, and the weather forecast was continually monitored as the sailors waited for the race to start. One by one, the sailboats moved to get in line for the race. What a sight to behold as they approached the starting line. The Bay was filled with boats with colorful spinnakers filling the horizon as the sailors waited patiently for the race to begin. You could feel the anticipation in the air.

Several minutes went by, but the race did not start. More moments passed, and the sailboats remained at the start line. After a while, we began to realize there was one small problem: There was no wind. Without the wind to fill its sails, a sailboat is powerless. So, the sailboats sat bobbing up and down in the waves but not going anywhere. Ultimately, that day's race had to be canceled. What a major disappointment! The time spent planning down to the last detail, the effort cleaning and preparing, the money paid to have the latest and greatest . . . it was all in vain, for without the wind, there was no sailing. I know I was disappointed, and I don't even own a sailboat. I can only imagine how the race participants felt. They had done all the work and gone to great lengths to prepare. But no amount of effort would change the fact that they had no wind to power their sailboats.

Have you ever experienced this in your life? You know you need to go somewhere, but you are powerless alone. This is particularly true when we need to make some changes. Most of us have habits that we want to change—those negative, repetitive behaviors that get in the way of our overall enjoyment of life. These habits keep us from evolving into better versions of ourselves. When we think of bad habits, we tend to think of physical ones like smoking, overeating, or not getting enough exercise.

But we can engage in a long list of bad habits. Perhaps your habit of choice is retail therapy when you're stressed, and your overdrawn credit cards prove that things need to change. Maybe you are plagued with procrastination and struggle to get anything done. Or you are always rushing because you struggle with time management. Mental habits like overthinking and dwelling on the past leave us emotionally drained. We can also be faced with addictions that not only hurt us but can destroy the lives of our loved ones. All these bad habits have one common denominator: They need to change.

Most of us struggle when trying to break those destructive tendencies. We begin with the determination to do things differently. We do well for a time until the storms of life hit. Then we fall back into the same behavior we wanted to eliminate, caught in an endless cycle of success and failure. The apostle Paul was familiar with this feeling, and he shared his frustration in a letter to the Romans. He said, "I don't really understand myself, for I want to do what is right, but I don't do it. Instead, I do what I hate" (Romans 7:15 NLT). Can you relate? We recognize that we need to change, but we find ourselves powerless to do so.

My sailboat story illustrates an essential spiritual principle: We cannot change ourselves, no matter how hard we try. Sheer willpower and determination are not enough to get us where we need to be. Like sailboats, we sit in the sea of life, bobbing up and down but going nowhere. We have no wind to fill our sails. The reality is that actual change can only come from God because he is our wind; he alone can give us the power to change.

When we try to change independently, our focus is usually on our outward behavior. But our behavior is determined by what is going on inside. God's focus transforms our entire being, not just our outward behavior. Actual change can only come from God because he wants to transform our inner being. Yes, he wants to fix those negative habits and behaviors, but he knows this begins with the motivation behind them. To help us, God gave us his Holy Spirit, who is the power behind our transformation. He is the wind that fills our sails.

John 15:5 gives another illustration: "I am the vine; you are the branches. If you remain in me and I in you, you will bear much fruit; apart from me you can do nothing." The late Dr. Charles Stanley, in his book *The Spirit-Filled Life*, explains.

> You are not equipped to produce change—only to bear it. . . . You are simply the vehicle through which it is expressed, as a branch is the vehicle through which the fruit-producing life of the vine is expressed. You are a bearer, not a producer. Branches are totally dependent on the vine for fruit. And we are totally dependent on the Holy Spirit.[31]

In an earlier chapter, we learned about the Holy Spirit's vital role in our transformation. We are complex beings. Our physical bodies are a network of nerves, blood vessels, muscles, and organs that give us life. But the physical is only one part. We have an inner spirit that is much more difficult to understand. What makes us do what we do? Why do we think in a particular way, and why do we hold onto certain beliefs and reject others? How can we handle deep emotions like love, hate, joy, and rage? How do we develop our attitudes and personality? The working of the inner person can be a great mystery to us and one we struggle to understand. But God fully understands the nuances of our temperaments, and the Holy Spirit can transform us to spiritual maturity and wholeness.

Part of the transformation process involves dealing with our sin problem. Paul struggled with doing things he did not want to do and not doing what he should have been doing. That nicely sums up our sin problem. On our own, sin tends to dictate our actions. We are often motivated by negative emotions such as selfishness, greed, and jealousy. The bottom line is that sin hurts us and those around us, but the Holy Spirit will transform us if we let him. He points out the sin in our lives to make us realize it's there. Too often, we become immune to sin and are unaware of the harm it causes us. The consequences of sin are like water. It fills us up and eventually flows to those around us. The reality is that our sin hurts us and can hurt those around us. The Holy Spirit's conviction helps us recognize the harm our actions cause.

I remember an incident when the Holy Spirit's conviction helped me recognize the damage that cruel words can cause. It began when I listened to gossip about a particular person. This led me to spread the rumor to others, and you can guess what came next. Soon, everyone in the group heard the rumor. Sadly, the rumor was not true, but it still did its damage. I saw the victim of this vicious gossip a few weeks later, and I felt terrible about what I had done. She was going through a tough breakup and was hurting. Instead of giving her comfort and encouragement, we added insult to injury by gossiping about her. I will never forget the look of devastation on her face. The Holy Spirit taught me a valuable lesson through my sin: Words hurt, and you can never take them back once they're spoken. When I'm tempted to gossip about someone, the Holy Spirit reminds me of the crushed look on this person's face, and it's enough for me to walk away.

Once we're willing to recognize the presence of sin, the Holy Spirit helps us to remove it from our lives. Like peeling the layers of an onion, the Holy Spirit will dig deeper into our inner selves to see what motivates sin. What is the thinking behind our sin? What is causing the impulse to engage in this harmful behavior? The root cause of sin is a breakdown of the inner man. A wound within our soul cannot be fixed with a bandage. If left untreated, this wound will fester and destroy us. The role of the Holy Spirit is to bring healing to these wounds and restore our spirit to health and wholeness.

Let's consider some essential points about transformation. First, this process is not something we earn or deserve. Transformation is based solely on the work of Jesus Christ on the cross. Because of Jesus's work, we can have the Holy Spirit dwell within us. The Holy Spirit brings about the necessary changes for our transformation. Second, our transformation does not happen overnight. It is a lifelong process because, as humans, we always have room for growth. But once the Holy Spirit begins the process, we can be assured that God will complete it. The Bible assures us, "I am sure that God Who began the good work in you will keep on working in you until the day Jesus Christ comes again" (Philippians 1:6 NLV).

We must also consider that the Holy Spirit's work will bear fruit in our lives. In other words, we will develop a godly character and a positive nature. These qualities are known in Scripture as the fruit of the Spirit. "But the Holy Spirit produces this kind of fruit in our lives: love, joy, peace, patience, kindness, goodness, faithfulness, gentleness, and self-control. There is no law against these things!" (Galatians 5:22–23 NLT).

Finally, our transformation requires us to do our part. We do not get to be passive passengers in life, but neither does the Holy Spirit take total control, leaving us zombies. God will never force his will on us. He works with and through us, not despite us. We do our part by consistently reading God's Word in the Bible to learn his truth and his will for our lives. Instead of trying to live by our strength, we let the Holy Spirit's strength, power, and wisdom shape our decisions and choices. The sailors in the regatta had a lot of preparation to do before the big race. They had to make sure their equipment was in proper working order. They needed to plot the course of the race and had to develop the best strategy to navigate it. They didn't just sit around, waiting for the wind. They prepared themselves to manage the wind once it arrived. The same is true for us. We must learn how to use the Holy Spirit's power to achieve the goals set before us to win the race of life.

As I have gotten older, I have come to recognize the benefit of hindsight. I can see God's hand in my life as he has transformed my being. In my younger years, I was arrogant and thought I had all the answers. I cringe to think about my attitude and how judgmental I could be. Although I was a believer, I was not always kind. I often was hyper-critical of the faults of others and blind to my shortcomings. I was gossiping and talking negatively about people behind their backs. I was quick to tear others down without regard for how my words demeaned them. I am not proud of the person I was back then.

Fortunately, the Holy Spirit was at work in my life, and he began to work on my attitude. He started within my inner being and addressed my attitude toward who I was. Growing up, I was the youngest of three, and I felt like an invisible child. My oldest sibling was rebellious, and my parents struggled with their behavior. The middle sibling in my family had special needs, and my parents' lives were filled with consulting professionals on how to best help him. So, when it came to me, my parents were just tired and had little energy to raise me. They expected me to stay out of trouble, get good grades, and not cause problems. Later in life, I now understand my parents' struggle. Raising children is not easy! But when I was younger, their lack of attention shaped my self-perception. All the energy and activity I put into gaining their attention went unnoticed. I was left with the feeling of never being good enough. I lacked self-confidence, and I certainly did not value myself.

The Holy Spirit began to show me that my critical spirit toward others stemmed from my lack of self-love. I thought I was unworthy of receiving love and attention, and I was taking that pain out on others. As I prayed and read God's Word, I saw myself in a new light. The Holy Spirit showed me that God loved me and that I had value in his eyes. He has always had time for me and, to this day, wants to spend time with me. He would never withhold his love from me, no matter what I did. And he has always loved me for who I am, not for what I have done for him. Seeing God as my perfect Father changed my sense of self-worth entirely. As I began to feel better about myself, I noticed I was treating others better. As I learned to love myself, I could truly love others. I was more patient and compassionate. I stopped gossiping and demeaning others and learned to put forth love.

This is how I know God is real. He has changed me for the better. The Holy Spirit has transformed me into someone I love and respect. I know that would never happen through my effort alone. I need the Holy Spirit's wind to fill my sails and carry me on the journey of a lifetime!

My sailing story has a happy ending. The very next day was windy. As I watched the sailors again prepare for the race, I saw the smiles on their faces. They finally had what they had been waiting for, the power to run their race. It was remarkable how these sailors monitored the winds and skillfully used their sails to harness the wind power to navigate through the water. I was astonished by how fast the boats moved, considering they were powered only by the wind. And the same is true of our lives. Amazing things will happen when we learn to open our hearts and minds to the power of the Holy Spirit.

CHAPTER 8

The End of the Road

At the beginning of our marriage, my husband and I needed to find clever and inexpensive forms of entertainment. We were saving money to buy a house and had a bare-bones budget with few luxuries. We did not have cable TV, so we were limited to the basic channels and PBS. That was when we discovered radio programs that were both entertaining and free. We would sit in the living room to listen to our shows, much like those from earlier generations when the radio was a household luxury. We enjoyed the lost art of listening to stories and using our imagination to fill in the pictures. I fondly remember those times and am happy that many of the stories can be heard today on podcasts.

One program that we loved was *The End of the Road Show*, narrated by Tom Bodett. The stories captured the essence of life in the small town of Homer, Alaska. Homer is a coastal town that is both charming and remote. It has been nicknamed "the end of the road" because it is located on a four-and-a-half-mile spit at the end of the Sterling Highway. Kachemak Bay surrounds the city, and its beauty is breathtaking.

Because of its remote location and small size, it would be easy to assume that not much happens in Homer. However, Tom Bodett dispelled that myth each week by telling a story about one of the many colorful residents. With his deep baritone voice and soothing speech, he would recount the quirky and humorous events within the town. We were captivated by Tom's storytelling skills as our minds painted the images of his spoken words. His tales were wholesome and humorous, giving us a glimpse of this charming town's color and vibrant life. The takeaway each week was that just because the road ends does not mean that life ends. And often, that life goes beyond anything we could have ever imagined.

There is a fantastic parallel between Tom's stories and the believer's life in Jesus Christ. We will reach the "end of the road" here on Earth when we die. But our life does not stop when we die because it continues in heaven. The life we enjoy there will be beyond anything we could have imagined.

Fortunately, the Bible gives us a glimpse of what happens after death and clarifies that our lives will continue. Everyone needs to recognize and understand what happens to us at that point. Our choices and how we live here on Earth will significantly impact how we spend eternity. I highly recommend the book *A Place Called Heaven* by Dr. Robert Jeffress.[32] Dr. Jeffress explains what the Bible says about our eternal home and what we can expect. I hope you will read the book, but I would like to highlight a few of his compelling points.

We first need to recognize that heaven is an actual, physical location. It is not a spiritual state of mind or a made-up utopia created by the human imagination. Humans naively think of heaven as a place where we exist as spiritual beings floating on clouds and playing the harp. Nothing could be further from the truth. Jesus gives us a description and an invitation in John 14:2–3. "There is more than enough room in my Father's home. If this were not so, would I have told you that I am going to prepare a place for you? When everything is ready, I will come and get you, so that you will always be with me where I am" (NLT).

We can glean a few things about heaven from these verses. First, Jesus describes rooms in his Father's house. This suggests that heaven is a physical place where people live. Jesus also states that he will prepare a place for us, meaning heaven is a tangible location. The idea that Jesus will prepare a place for us and then will later return to Earth and take us home with him suggests that heaven is indeed a location, and it exists in a completely different dimension from Earth.[33]

What is heaven like? Jesus answers that question in his reply to the thief who was crucified beside him as he hung on the cross. "And Jesus replied, 'I assure you, today you will be with me in paradise'" (Luke 23:43 NLT).

Think of all the beautiful places here on Earth that we consider paradise. Imagine the stunning beaches of Curacao or the glorious mountains of Switzerland. Their beauty is magnificent, and they are often considered paradise on Earth. Yet they will pale in comparison to the splendor of heaven. Heaven is so much more than a beautiful location; it is a place of perfect peace and harmony. The Bible describes heaven as a place where "'the wolf and the lamb will feed together, and the lion will eat straw like the ox, and dust will be the serpent's food. They will neither harm nor destroy on all my holy mountain,' says the Lord" (Isaiah 65:25).

Heaven is also a place without tears or pain. The book of Revelation comforts us with these words: "He will wipe every tear from their eyes. There will be no more death or mourning or crying or pain, for the old order of things has passed away" (Revelation 21:4).

The greatest thing about heaven is that we will know that we are finally home, and this is the place where we truly belong. Dr. Ray Pritchard, president of Keep Believing Ministries, writes,

> Sometimes, we discuss a "God-shaped vacuum" inside the human heart. I believe there is also a "heaven-shaped vacuum," a sense that we were made for something more than this life. We were made to live forever somewhere. In a real sense, we were made for heaven.[34]

When talking about heaven, it is essential to recognize that heaven and Earth will be joined one day. In Revelation 21–22, John describes a new heaven and Earth with a New Jerusalem between the two. At some point, God will destroy the Earth as we know it today. It saddens me to think that all the good things we enjoy here on Earth will be destroyed. But its destruction is necessary because sin has so corrupted our physical environment that God needs to create a better version without the mark of sin. The new Earth will be a familiar place because it will hold everything we enjoy about Earth now. Much of the new Earth will be like our current Earth. The most significant difference is that the curse of sin will have been lifted, and we will be able to enjoy life as God created it.[35]

Heaven is something we long for deep in our inner being. But how can we be assured that when we die, we will go to heaven? Jesus has done the work on the cross. He died to pay the penalty for our sins. He did for us what we could not do for ourselves. His death and resurrection have paved the way for us to have right standing before God. Jesus's sacrifice allows us to enter a personal relationship with God, our Creator.

Remember, God has given us free will, and whether or not we accept what Jesus has done on our behalf is a choice. If we are willing to admit that we are sinners and accept what Jesus has done on our behalf by choosing to believe what the Bible says, then we can enjoy a relationship with God. Through the same deliberate choice, we are promised a life in heaven. This truth resonates throughout the Bible, especially in the Gospels. John 6:47 says, "Very truly I tell you, the one who believes has eternal life."

But it is not enough to know what it says. We must deliberately choose to believe it. The Bible is clear; Jesus's work on the cross saves those who believe in him. There is nothing we can do to earn our place in heaven. Even if we think we are good people and do all the right things, we will never be good enough to be redeemed by our merit. We will always fall short, and the doors of heaven will be closed to us.

The good news is that we do not need to be good enough. Our hope of eternal life is available to anyone who chooses to receive Christ. Some say that this truth is narrow-minded and intolerant because it means that there is only one way to get to heaven. Many are more comfortable with the idea that all religions lead to heaven. But that is not true. Jesus tells us, "I am the way, the truth, and the life. No one can come to the Father except through me" (John 14:6 NLT).

Here is a foundational biblical truth: Jesus is the key to a relationship with God and a home in heaven. Humans cannot do what Jesus did for us. Religion and enlightenment will not remove the stain of sin. All are invited to come to him, and his offer is free. The hope of heaven is extended to us by the grace of God, and it is available to everyone willing to receive it. It all comes down to the choices we make. Do we believe in Jesus and accept his offer or reject it entirely and deny the truth?

What will life in heaven be like? The Bible gives us some glimpses into eternity, and while God does not explain everything in precise detail, we can get a little taste of what we can expect. I believe God gives us the correct amount of information about what heaven will be like. If he gave us too much, our human minds couldn't grasp it. Second, if we truly understood what heaven is like, we would not want to stay here on Earth. But God also needs to give us the hope of heaven and the promise of a better life to help us get through our lives here on Earth.

We must understand that our Earthly life is not all there is and that God has plans for us that extend into eternity. God also needs to dispel all our false preconceived notions of heaven. I often think about how heaven is depicted in our culture. We often think of heaven as floating in the clouds, playing a harp. We think we will have crowns on our heads and wings as we aimlessly float around without purpose or meaning. Or we have the misconception that heaven will be one long, unending church service. If you ask me about these ideas, they sound monotonous and boring. And it is a far cry from all that heaven will be like.

Life in heaven will be different from our life on Earth in that we will no longer be under the curse of sin and its devastating hold on us. There will be no pain, heartache, disappointment, or sadness. We will have the joy of God's presence, and our lives will be filled with peace, contentment, and fulfillment because we are finally where we belong.

We will also be given new bodies that will not wear out and cause pain. While we are indeed spiritual beings, we also exist here on Earth in physical form. In the New Testament, we see some indication that we will indeed have new bodies in heaven.

> It will happen in a moment, in the blink of an eye, when the last trumpet is blown. For when the trumpet sounds, those who have died will be raised to live forever. And we who are living will also be transformed (1 Corinthians 15:52 NLT).

> But our citizenship is in heaven. And we eagerly await a Savior from there, the Lord Jesus Christ, who, by the power that enables him to bring everything under his control, will transform our lowly bodies so that they will be like his glorious body (Philippians 3:20–21).

Thomas's encounter with Jesus following his resurrection also supports the idea that we will have physical bodies in heaven. After Jesus's death and burial, Thomas was clearly confused and full of doubts, which was understandable. It wasn't until Thomas had a physical body to feel and probe that his doubts were erased. "Then [Jesus] said to Thomas, 'Put your finger here; see my hands. Reach out your hand and put it into my side. Stop doubting and believe'" (John 20:27).

Jesus also appeared to his other followers in bodily form, then he ascended to heaven in the same body. "Then Jesus led them to Bethany, and lifting his hands to heaven, he blessed them. While he was blessing them, he left them and was taken up to heaven" (Luke 24:50–51 NLT).

How will we occupy our time in heaven? The Bible indicates that we will engage in two primary activities: worship and work. The apostle John's vision enlightens us with the heavenly worship of God that is continually taking place. "And I heard every creature in heaven and on Earth and under the Earth and in the sea, and all that is in them, saying, 'To him who sits on the throne and to the Lamb be blessing and honor and glory and might forever and ever!'" (Revelation 5:13 ESV). One day, we will be able to participate in this momentous service.

This worship service will be beyond anything we have seen on Earth. Think about a multitude gathered to honor God, the collective voices joining together to give honor, gratitude, and praise to our Maker. Imagine the sound that such worship will make. And we will be there! We will also have the pleasure of being face-to-face with Jesus. Dwell on this for a moment. We will be in the presence of Jesus! How different will our worship be when we see him? I doubt we would offer simple lip service to the King of kings. Our hearts will be ablaze with praise as we stand in his presence. We will freely express the adoration of our hearts because it is part of our makeup. It is ingrained within us because we were created to worship God.

Our activities in heaven will not be limited to worship. We will have responsibilities. Heaven will not be a retirement community where we live out our golden years. We were not created to sit around and do nothing. The idea of working in heaven is foreign to many people. Yet, Scripture teaches that when God created Adam, he "took the man and put him in the Garden of Eden to work it and take care of it" (Genesis 2:15). Work was part of the original Eden, part of a perfect human life.[36] God is also a worker, as seen in the creation story. And he continues to work to this day. In the Gospel of John, Jesus tells us, "My Father is always working, and so am I" (John 5:17 NLT).

From the creation story, we can see that work gives God great pleasure as he stops to admire his work and declares, "It is good!" (Genesis 1:9 NIV). Work allows God to express his character and love. His work is an extension of himself, magnifying his goodness, kindness, and love. Since we are created in his image, our work can reflect who we are, and it is something we can enjoy.

The idea of having a job in heaven might make some of us moan with grief. Returning to the monotonous daily grind of working is not something we look forward to. The good news is that a job in heaven will be a different experience. Remember that in this world, we are under sin's curse, and as part of the curse, our work is laborious, intensive, and often tedious. Without sin's curse, we will find our work both exhilarating and enjoyable. The work God has prepared for us will be instantly rewarding, constantly refreshing, and ideally suited for who we were created to be. This work will be eminently satisfying and give us a sense of purpose. Our jobs will be acts of worship that will bring glory to God. Our worship is not limited to sitting in a pew singing hymns on Sunday morning. My favorite definition of worship is a continual awareness of, gratitude toward, and submission to God in everything we do. We worship God while we do everything else.[37]

Then, like God in the creation story, we will take time out to rest. However, we do not need to stop working because we are exhausted or need a break from work to do something we enjoy. We will rest from our jobs so that we can take the time to reflect on what we have done and enjoy the fruits of our labor. Our work will give us great satisfaction and contentment because what we do will result in something good. Perhaps we will follow in our Father's footsteps as we create beautiful things. Or we will become cultivators like Adam and Eve and take the time to enjoy the bounty of our harvest. Every task performed in heaven, no matter how big or small, will be for the collective good of all. As we carry out our roles in heaven, we will find great contentment because our work will give meaning to our lives and a sense of belonging.

Life in heaven will not be limited to worship and work. Just like Adam and Eve, who walked with God in the evenings, we will spend time with him, getting to know him better. We will also enjoy time with all the other believers in heaven. We are part of God's large family and will enjoy community with them.

While we will all enjoy the experience of heaven, we will not all receive the same reward. We know that our admission into heaven won't be based on anything we do. It is based on the work of Christ and whether we are willing to accept his gift of salvation. However, our reward in heaven will be given according to our work on Earth. This fact is spelled out in the parable of the minas found in Luke 19:11–27. This parable tells the story of a nobleman who entrusts his servants with money while he goes on a journey. When he returns, he evaluates their actions and rewards them accordingly. The faithful servants wisely used the resources they had been given and increased their value. The foolish servant squandered the opportunity by holding on to the money. In the end, the faithful servants were given more based on how well they used what they had been given. The foolish servant not only did not receive a reward, but the minas he received were taken away and given to those who were faithful.

This applies to our life in heaven. How we choose to spend our life here on Earth matters, and it will significantly impact our future lives. Everything we do and how we treat others is of great importance to God, and one day we will stand before him and be held accountable for our actions. Every good deed, no matter how small, will be noticed. Every time we treat someone with kindness and respect, even when they are unkind to us, will also matter. God will evaluate all our thoughts, motives, actions, and words.

Our loving Savior, the Lord Almighty, will be the final judge of good and evil done on this Earth. Yes, he will punish the guilty and extinguish sin forever. But he will also reward the actions of the faithful. They will come to light in God's presence, and he will reward us accordingly. I don't know about you, but this has become my life's motivation so that I can one day hear these words from God's lips: "Well done, good and faithful servant!"

When we reach "the end of the road" of our life here on Earth, we can be assured that there is a beautiful new life ahead of us in eternity with God. This life is only available through accepting what Jesus has done for us on the cross. We cannot earn our way to heaven by being good people. Heaven is a gift we receive when we trust Jesus to save us. We are saved by God's grace, and we never have to worry about being "good enough" to go to heaven. Heaven is God's promise to all believers, and God keeps his promises. What a blessing to know that when our life draws to a close here on Earth, the best is yet to come!

CHAPTER 9

Two Sides of the Same Coin

My in-laws were blessed with many opportunities to travel all over the world. They had countless adventures journeying to each continent, exploring the unique cultures and lifestyles within the landscape. They would captivate my children with their stories of faraway places. Often, they would give the boys a coin or two from the places they visited, and they had fun examining the inscriptions. Each coin had symbols unique to that country's history, culture, and personality, and provided hints of what life was like there. The coins also gave insight into what the people of that region found important. For example, many American coins have some form of the word *freedom* or *liberty* on them. The United States is a country that enjoys the blessings of great freedoms.

For the most part, we use coins as currency to exchange for goods and services. However, the coin also has a role in decision-making. It's used often in the "coin toss," a fun and easy way to make key decisions. For example, heads or tails are the deciding factor at the start of every

Super Bowl. Flipping the coin is significant because there is a random, and therefore equal, chance for either side to land upward. And the decision is final.

It is the same with our spiritual life. We can be for or against God, but we cannot be both. It is just not possible. At the close of this book, each reader has an important decision to make. Do you believe God and all he says? Are you willing to walk daily with him? Or do you wish to reject God and do your own thing? Your future depends on this decision, and it's a choice only you can make. No one can do it for you. And you only have two sides of a coin to consider. Are you for God or against him?

Israel was faced with this decision at the base of Mount Sinai. In the account found in Exodus 32, we read that Moses had left the camp to meet with God and left Aaron in charge of the people. It was during that meeting with God that Moses received the Ten Commandments. Moses had been away from camp for forty days, and the people of Israel started to panic. They wondered if Moses had abandoned them, leaving them stranded in the hot desert.

God was using this extended absence to test the faithfulness of his people. Would they remember all the things God had done for them? Would they remember the dry ground they walked on as God parted the Red Sea so they could escape? As they ate their manna, would they cling to the hope that God would continue to provide for them? Could they remain steadfast in God's promise of a land flowing with milk and honey?

It was a test that Israel failed. Despite all that God had done for them, the people turned against God and Moses. They chose to take matters into their own hands, and they created a golden calf which they could worship instead of their God. When Moses came down the mountain, he found the camp dancing before this idol made by their own hands.

Israel was trying to have both sides of the coin. They wanted to enjoy the benefits that God gave them. They were eager to enter the Promised Land so they could enjoy the blessings found there. But whenever life got tough, they reverted to their old ways. Instead of worshiping the living God, they chose to worship an idol made from metal.

The children of Israel were trying to have a life with God and his promises, and at the same time, they wanted to do their own thing. It simply was not possible because they are two sides of the same coin. And you cannot have both. God forgave Israel once they confessed their wrongdoing. But their actions were not without consequences. "And the Lord struck the people with a plague because of what they did with the calf Aaron had made" (Exodus 32:35). The plague served as a reminder that Israel could not truly serve God and have one foot still in their old way of life without God.

We are also faced with the same temptation. God's way of life appeals to us, especially the benefits. But sometimes God's way is hard and requires work. We are tempted to find the easy way out and take matters into our own hands. And that does not work. Either we are for God or we are against him. Either we trust him and his plan or we don't. Either we believe what he says is true or we doubt him. Either we follow him wholeheartedly or we rebel against his goodness. There is no gray area in these matters.

The following quote appropriately sums up our discussion:

> I hear references to grey areas, but they don't apply to life and godliness. There are simply two sides to the coin: good or evil, life or death, Heaven or hell, and it takes walking with

109

God always (not intellect or culture) to choose right. One side cost Jesus the cross, and the other will cost us eternity. We are all limited to trusting God or satisfying our desires. We either walk with God or walk alone. Even in death, there's no hovering around the galaxies or swimming in oblivion because our choice now will determine where we end.[38]

When we choose God and live for him, we can expect the many benefits we have explored in this book. God freely offers this life to us, which was made possible by Christ's work on the cross. The work has been done. All we need to do is accept the offer, and we can experience a whole new way of living, enjoying the many benefits of having a relationship with God.

We now need to take a moment to consider the other side of the coin. Life on this side differs drastically from the other. Yes, we will have great freedom to do as we please. We can do our own thing and follow our rules as we see fit. We can choose our destiny and pursue a life that fulfills all our longings and desires. Life can be all about us and getting what we want out of it. We can use the free will that God has given us to do our own thing and not engage in a relationship with him. But at what cost?

Choosing to live independently of God means that the quality of our lives depends solely on us. We are on our own. We do not have God's resources to tap into, nor does his presence guide us. Sin will keep us from all the good things God offers us. And upon our death, we will not receive eternal life with God.

As I close out this book, I invite you to consider these options. I hope with all my heart that you will embrace a life with God. It begins with a simple prayer:

> God, I believe you, and I recognize my need for you. I choose to accept what Jesus Christ has done for me on the cross, and I recognize that I cannot save myself from my sin, so I accept your gracious invitation into your family.

I pray that as you begin your new life in Christ, you will experience his great peace, joy, and contentment in all that you do. I pray that God will lead you into a life of purpose where you can share his love and care for those who are less fortunate with kindness and respect. Finally, I pray that you will live daily with the joyful hope of heaven and the sure knowledge that when life here on Earth is finished, all of us who believe will finally see our Lord Jesus face to face and live forever with him.

Endnotes

1   Rebecca Hagelin, "Christian Faith in American History," Focus on the Family, July 2, 2024, https://www.focusonthefamily.com/parenting/christian-faith-in -american-history/.

2   Hagelin, "Christian Faith in American History."

3   Michelle Anderson, "George Washington," Faith of Our Fathers, accessed September 24, 2025, https://faithofourfathers.net/george-washington.html.

4   Michelle Anderson, "James Madison," Faith of Our Fathers, accessed September 24, 2025, https://faithofourfathers.net/james-madison.html.

5   Michelle Anderson, "Patrick Henry," Faith of Our Fathers, accessed September 24, 2025, https://faithofourfather /patrick-henry.html.

6   Gallup, "How Many Americans Believe in God?" Gallup.com, June 24, 2022, https://news.gallup.com/poll/268205/American.believe-god.aspx.

7   Lydia Saad, "Americans' Ratings of U.S. Professions Stay Historically Low," Gallup.com, March 27, 2025, https://news.gallup.com/poll/655106/americans -ratings-professions-stay-historically-low.aspx.

8   Ronald Inglehart, "World Values Survey Association," WVS Database, February 20, 2021, https://www.worldvaluessurvey.org/WVSNewsShow.jsp?ID=421.

9   Inglehart, "World Values Survey Association."

10   Daniel A. Cox, "The Decline of Religion in American Family Life," American Enterprise Institute, December 11, 2019, https://www.aei.org/research-products /report/the-decline-of-religion-in-american-family-life/.

11   Cox, "The Decline of Religion in American Family Life."

12   Cox, "The Decline of Religion in American Family Life."

13   "Popular Quotes," Goodreads, accessed August 8, 2025, https://www
.goodreads.com/quotes.

14   Melanie Campbell, "15 Powerful Bible Verses About God's Sovereignty," Bible
Study Tools, May 3, 2020, https://www.biblestudytools.com/bible-study/topical
-studies/powerful-verses-to-remind-us-of-gods-sovereignty.html.

15   Warren W. Wiersbe, *Be Counted: Living a Life That Counts for God* (Colorado
Springs: David C. Cook, 2010), 184.

16   Wiersbe, *Be Counted*, 183.

17   Wiersbe, *Be Counted*, 183.

18   Joyce Meyer, *The Power of Simple Prayer* (New York, NY: Faith Words,
2007), 11.

19   *Names of God* (Peabody, MA: Rose Publishing, 2003).

20   Paul Bubna, "The Holy Spirit Our Helper," sermon, September 6, 1987.

21   "Oak Island Mystery," Wikipedia Foundation, last updated September
6, 2025, https://en.wikipedia.org/w/index.php?title=Oak_Island_
mystery&oldid=1299392431.

22   Mary Whitfield Roeloffs, "History Channel's 'Curse of Oak Island' Draws
Millions of Viewers—Beating Almost Everything Else on Cable," *Forbes*, February
20, 2024, https://www.forbes.com/sites/maryroeloffs/2023/12/07/history-channels
-curse-of-oak-island-draws-millions-of-viewers-beating-almost-everything-else
-on-cable/?sh=672eb4324d9d.

23   Shirley Alarie, "4 Parable of the Hidden Treasure Lessons," Finding God
Among Us, August 6, 2025, https://findinggodamongus.com/parable-of-the
-hidden-treasure-lessons/.

24   Alarie, "4 Parable of the Hidden Treasure Lessons."

25   Justin Taylor, "The Pattern of the Kingdom: 'God's People, in God's Place,
Under God's Rule,'" The Gospel Coalition, October 29, 2017, https://www
.thegospelcoalition.org/blogs/justin-taylor/the-pattern-of-the-kingdom-gods
-people-in-gods-place-under-gods-rule/.

26   "How Can We Walk in God's Ways (Psalm 128:1)?" GotQuestions.org, February 9, 2023, https://www.gotquestions.org/walk-in-Gods-ways.html.

27   Rick Warren, *The Purpose Driven Life* (Grand Rapids: Zondervan, 2002), 23.

28   Warren Wiersbe, *Be Worshipful* (Colorado Springs: Cook Communications Ministries, 2004), 21.

29   Wiersbe, *Be Worshipful*, 21.

30   "What Does 'Shalom' Mean?" Bible Hub, accessed August 18, 2025, https://biblehub.com/q/what_does_'shalom'_mean.htm.

31   Charles F. Stanley, *The Spirit-Filled Life: Discover the Joy of Surrendering to the Holy Spirit* (Nashville: Nelson Books, 2014), 74.

32   Robert Jeffress, *A Place Called Heaven: 10 Surprising Truths About Your Eternal Home* (Grand Rapids: Baker Books, 2018).

33   Jeffress, *A Place Called Heaven*, 29–30.

34   Keep Believing Ministries, "What Is Heaven like? Top Questions Answered with Bible Quotes," Bible Study Tools, April 19, 2020, https://www.biblestudytools.com/bible-study/topical-studies/what-is-heaven-like-11636670.html.

35   Jeffress, *A Place Called Heaven*, 36–39.

36   Randy Alcorn, "9 Facts about Heaven That Will Surprise You," Lifeway, July 9, 2025, https://www.lifeway.com/en/articles/facts-about-heaven.

37   Jeffress, *A Place Called Heaven*, 95.

38   Martha Olawale, "Two Sides to the Coin—God or Not God," Abiding Christian, October 30, 2023, https://www.abidingchristian.com/blog/two-sides-to-the-coingod-or-not-god.

About the Author

Meet Christine Krulan, a seasoned instructor of women's Bible studies with over twenty years of experience. Christine's passion for teaching is matched only by her love of reading, having delved into the writings of renowned theologians such as Dallas Willard, E. Stanley Jones, Charles Stanley, A.W. Tozer, Rick Warren, C.S. Lewis, and Eugene Edwards. Her extensive studies have provided her with a robust theological foundation, enabling her to share profound and compassionate insights into the journey of faith.

Outside of teaching and studying, Christine cherishes the time she spends with her husband and two adult sons at their home in North Carolina. She thrives in the great outdoors, relishing activities like hiking, gardening, and kayaking. Additionally, she delights in training her two adorable Cavalier King Charles Spaniels, Buzz and Rex, and proudly showcases their skills in agility competitions.

Christine's mission is to inspire others with her love for faith, family, and furry friends, and to continue reflecting God's light with enthusiasm and joy.

www.ingramcontent.com/pod-product-compliance
Lightning Source LLC
Chambersburg PA
CBHW020319130626
46549CB00003B/938